Plays: Four

# Elektra, Orestes, Iphigeneia in Tauris

*Elektra*, *Orestes* and *Iphigeneia in Tauris* show the consequences of Agamemnon's 'sacrifice' of his daughter at the start of the Trojan War. Originally written for separate occasions, they were performed together as *Agamemnon's Children* at the Gate Theatre, London, in 1995.

'Euripides, the Athenian playwright who dared to question the whims of wanton gods, has always been the most intriguing of the Greek tragedians. Now, with translations aimed at the stage rather than the page, his restless intellect strikes the chord it always should have. This revivification is due in part to the translations of Kenneth McLeish, whose skill at rendering "spoken" (rather than "written") dialogue is masterly . . . Together this non-trilogy constitutes a remarkable achievement both in itself and in reclaiming Euripides as a playwright whose works are still gloriously alive.' *Evening Standard*

'Translation which swings from armchair idiom to a windswept poetic spareness, without ever losing its sense of purpose.' *Guardian*

The volume is introduced by J. Michael Walton, series editor of the Methuen Classical Greek Dramatists, and by Kenneth McLeish.

**Euripides** was born near Athens between 485 and 480 BC and grew up during the years of Athenian recovery after the Persian Wars. His first play was presented in 455 BC and he wrote some hundred altogether. Nineteen survive – a greater number than those of Aeschylus and Sophocles combined – including *Alkestis*, *Medea*, *Bacchae*, *Hippolytos*, *Ion* and *The Women of Troy*. His later plays are marked by a sense of disillusion at the futility of human aspiration which amounts on occasion to a philosophy of absurdism. A year or two before his death he left Athens to live at the court of the King of Macedon, dying there in 406 BC.

# EURIPIDES

# Plays: Four

**Elektra**

**Orestes**

**Iphigeneia in Tauris**

*translated by Kenneth McLeish*

*introduced by J. Michael Walton
and Kenneth McLeish*

series editor: J. Michael Walton

METHUEN DRAMA

# METHUEN CLASSICAL GREEK DRAMATISTS

This collection first published in Great Britain 1997
by Methuen Drama
Random House, 20 Vauxhall Bridge Road, London SW1V 2SA
and Australia, New Zealand and South Africa
and Auckland, Melbourne, Singapore and Toronto
and distributed in the United States of America
by Heinemann, a division of Reed Elsevier Inc.
361 Hanover Street, Portsmouth, New Hampshire
NH 03801 3959

*Elektra, Orestes, Iphigeneia in Tauris* translations copyright
© 1997 by Kenneth McLeish

This collection copyright © 1997 by Methuen Drama
Editor's Introduction copyright © 1997 by J. Michael Walton
Translator's Introduction copyright © 1997 by
Kenneth McLeish

The authors and translator have asserted their moral rights

ISBN 0-413-71630-9

Random House UK Limited Reg. No. 954009

A CIP catalogue record for this book
is available from the British Library

Typeset by Wilmaset Ltd, Birkenhead, Wirral
Printed and bound in Great Britain by
Cox & Wyman Ltd, Reading, Berkshire

## Caution
All rights whatsoever in these translations are strictly reserved.
Application for performance, etc., should be made before
rehearsals begin to the translator's agent: Alan Brodie
Representation Ltd, 211 Piccadilly, London W1V 9LD. No
performance may be given unless a licence has been obtained.

This paperback is sold subject to the condition that it shall not,
by way of trade or otherwise, be lent, resold, hired out or
otherwise circulated without the publisher's prior consent in any
form of binding or cover other than that in which it is published
and without a similar condition including this condition being
imposed on the subsequent purchaser.

# CONTENTS

# EDITOR'S INTRODUCTION

Dating anything in the classical period is an imprecise art. This is in part the result of sketchy records. If the Greeks did record major events they tended to do it either by referring to the period of office of a particular chief *archon* or by dating it back to the first Olympiad in 776 BC. This latter practice was introduced by the historian Timaeus who was not born until fifty years after Sophocles and Euripides had died. Records for the dramatic festivals were preserved on lists carved in stone, known as the *didaskaliai*, which recorded the names of winning playwrights and prize-winning actors as well as the name of the *choregos*, the private citizen with responsibility for any financial commitments to a set of productions which went beyond what was supplied by the state.

Aristotle was eventually to draw up his own *didaskaliai* and later grammarians and historians were to make use of these in their records. Most of the original stone records have disappeared and Aristotle's lists are at best fragmentary. The result of all this is that most evidence for when plays were performed is haphazard. As the play texts have survived in largely the same way, it can be regarded as good fortune rather than bad that we have firm dates for five of the seven Aeschylus plays which have survived; two of the seven Sophocles; and eight of the nineteen Euripides. The fact that three of these, Sophocles' *Oedipus at Colonus*, and Euripides' *Iphigeneia at Aulis* and *Bacchae*, were all performed posthumously makes it more difficult to trace influences and stylistic characteristics. It is even more difficult to relate incidents, in what was always a largely topical dramatic form, to specific historical events.

This is more of a problem for other plays than those featured in the present volume but a corollary is that we know precious little about the playwrights themselves. The later biographies are sketchy and seem to rely on evidence as wayward as the plays of Aristophanes who used Euripides as a character in three plays, but was more concerned with a good gag than accurate character-study. Euripides, according to most sources, was born sometime around 480 BC. One reason for the doubt is that the best authority for this date has more than a whiff of convenience to it. Many later chroniclers tended to follow the principle established by the first Greek historian Herodotus for whom mere fact was not allowed to get in the way of a good story. The Athenians made a great deal of capital, literally as well as metaphorically, out of the defeat of the Persians at the Battle of Salamis in 480 BC. On that day, a later record has it, Aeschylus fought in the battle, Sophocles sung in the victory choir and Euripides was born.

Allowing ourselves the licence to accept this momentous birthday – perhaps the circumstances of his birth contributed to his reputed fondness for writing his plays on Salamis – let us also look forward to the year 458 BC. Aeschylus was now elderly but all the plays of his which have survived are from the last part of his life. None of them shows any sign of diminishing powers. Aeschylus was to die in 456 in Sicily, not of old age, but as a result of a freak accident. In 458 he produced for the festival of the Great Dionysia a group of plays which have subsequently been regarded as one of the supreme achievements of all theatre. The *Oresteia* is a trilogy whose subject is the return of Agamemnon from Troy to his native Argos, his subsequent murder at the hands of his wife Klytemnestra, the vengeance of his son Orestes on Klytenestra and her lover Aigisthos and, in the last play of the three, Orestes' trial in Athens for matricide and his subsequent acquittal. There was a fourth play, a farcical satyr play, as was the custom, but that was not handed down alongside the trilogy.

The *Oresteia* is a founding document of European drama. It is also a wonderful piece of theatre. What had been intended for a single performance only on one day in March 458 BC, one production being the most that any playwright could expect, became an immediate reference point, a yardstick by which subsequent tragedy was to be judged. To Aeschylus was awarded the singular accolade that his plays could be offered in revival at subsequent festivals. Attending that first performance, if we allow our fancy to run its course, was a twenty-one-year-old Euripides, a budding writer for whom Aeschylus represented what was staid and old-fashioned, not perhaps in the message of the trilogy because the *Oresteia* gives every impression of supporting the infant democratic system, but in the language of theatre. Here were long speeches and even longer choruses; here was language that no one had ever spoken in the Assembly, never mind on the streets of Athens; here was an acceptance of the conventions of theatre that were poetic to the point of being ridiculous.

Whatever the sentiments of a piece, how could an audience take seriously a recognition scene between brother and sister based on a similarity of hair and footprints, and then confirm it with some woven piece of cloth? Three Great Dionysias on, Aeschylus was dead and Euripides began his own career as a playwright. It was years before he gained any success and years more before he was to produce his stage response to Aeschylus' *Oresteia*. The exact date of Euripides' *Elektra* is one we do not know. The usual view is that it was from about 414 BC because of an apparent reference to the Sicilian Expedition of that year from the god Kastor in his final speech. This is flimsy evidence and there is no real knowing whether Euripides may not have been triggered just as much by the *Elektra* of Sophocles, which also duplicates the time-scale and incidents of *Choephoroi*, the middle play of the *Oresteia*.

What is beyond dispute is that this was where Euripides set the record straight over the recognition between Orestes and Elektra which Aeschylus had engineered less by logic than by dramatic necessity. Euripides' *Elektra* is no downtrodden princess, lamenting her life away in the palace, at the mercy of a vicious mother. She has been married off to a yeoman farmer and lives with him in their cottage close to the Argive border. Orestes arrives incognito with Pylades but, rather than introduce himself to his sister and enlist her help in the vengeance to be visited on his mother and her lover, he is at pains to avoid her finding out who he is. Her husband has invited the guests to a meal and Elektra makes him send for the old shepherd who rescued Orestes as a child. Elektra still has no idea that this evasive man who claims to bring news of Orestes really is Orestes. When the Old Man turns up Orestes and Pylades are still indoors. His news is that someone has poured libations at Agamemnon's tomb and he suggests that it may be Orestes making a secret visit. Now, after all these years, here is the realist Euripides taking mocking revenge on Aeschylus. 'Try the hair against your own,' says the Old Man, 'See if the colour matches. Brother and sister: it might, it happens' (ll. 520–22). Elektra's scorn is merciless,

> . . . how could they match?
> His hair's an athlete's, a gentleman's,
> Hard and strong; mine's a woman's,
> Soft with combing. (ll. 527–30)

The Old Man tries again:

> The footprints, in the dust, beside the grave:
> Go there, match them against yours.
> ELEKTRA. There's no dust there. It's rock.
> And how could our footprints match –
> A man's, a woman's? His feet would be bigger.
> OLD MAN. You're right. We'll not recognise him that
>     way.
> I know! He'll be wearing some garment
> You made for him years ago,
> I smuggled him to safety in.
> ELEKTRA. When Orestes went into exile, I was a little
>     girl.
> Even if I had made him a 'garment',
> He was a child then. It'd hardly fit him now –
> Unless by some miracle, it grew while he did.
> (ll. 532–44)

So much for Aeschylus. This is a widely quoted scene not least for the light it throws on the theatrical method of the two playwrights. The contrast in styles is one around which Aristophanes will later write a whole comedy when he contrives a meeting in Hades between the two playwrights in *Frogs*. There, the newly dead Euripides encounters the fifty-years-dead Aeschylus and competes with him to decide who is the better dramatist, or rather, who will best serve the state by returning to the war-torn Athens, Aeschylus the warrior poet or Euripides the arch-realist. Possessing the two recognition scenes means that this is a competition in which we today can join. And because there can be no possible doubt that Euripides in *Elektra* was drawing the attention of his audience to the parallel scene in Aeschylus, it is perfectly legitimate to make a number of inferences about the rest of the play.

Orestes has plenty of opportunity to reveal himself to his sister. He goes as far as to admit that that is why he has come to Argos. He checks that the Chorus are friendly. Still he holds back. The whole tenor of the play invites us to consider why. This is not simply a modern and anachronistic reading of an ancient text. Still less is it an admission that Euripides was an inconsistent playwright. Quite the reverse. His consistency is impeccable. It is Elektra who is illogical. When Orestes first sees her he notes her shorn head. When she refers here to her hair 'soft with combing', we know it cannot be true. Licence is given to the audience to pick up on her claims to be friendless when the Chorus constantly offer friendship; to have to do menial tasks when there are slaves to do the work for her; to wear rags when she is doing so by choice and rejects the offer of a dress from the Chorus. Perhaps, and here we do reach a point of interpretation, Orestes' reluctance to reveal himself to the sister he has come to find is because of the sister he actually does find. Elektra admits to expecting a different Orestes from what she gets. He finds something far different from what he bargained for.

The only problem with all this is that the play, thus addressed, begins to invite all manner of other possibilities. But then, why not? Do not the lines suggest that Klytemnestra is as pleasant as Euripides can make her, a woman who was responsible for her husband's death but now regrets it and is making amends by attending her daughter after childbirth? Why not emphasise the uncomfortable position of Elektra's husband to whom she has been married off so that she will not have children who might embarrass the royal family? That much is spelt out when the Farmer informs the audience in the prologue that he has not slept with Elektra. As if this were not enough, Elektra makes sure that everyone else knows she is still a virgin, including two total strangers about whom she knows nothing except that they claim to have a message from her brother.

At one level the Farmer simply serves a dramatic function. He provides a reason for Elektra's living away from the palace; he is a token of her loss of status; he supplies the common touch, along with the Old Man, to a story which is about the ruling classes but ruling classes whose conduct affects everyone. Euripides here does take a leaf out of Aeschylus' book. The same device is used in the *Oresteia* with the Watchman who introduces the whole trilogy and the Nurse who arrives in *Choephoroi* with her recollections of Orestes as a baby. Euripides' farmer also has a pronounced and defined personality. He gives some insight into the real nature of Elektra, her determined martyrdom, her obsessions, her difficulty in distinguishing between reality and fantasy. The Elektra whom the Farmer has to live with claims to applaud his virtue but turns on him like a fishwife when he does the decent thing by offering the strangers hospitality: 'What are you playing at, asking them in like that? They're men of rank' (ll. 405–7). Such a response gives an added frisson to Elektra's statement that the strangers have arrived 'To see how I am, how I suffer' and the Farmer's response, 'And what they haven't seen, you've told them' (ll. 355–6). His basic decency is commented upon with surprise by Orestes:

> It just goes to show, we should never judge
> Other people by what they look like.
> Character matters more than appearance.
> Kings' sons can be worthless,
> Moral pigmies can breed giants,
> A coward wear silks and satins, a hero rags. (ll. 366–71)

What is something of a platitude in Orestes' mouth can be read as encapsulating Euripides' writing style. Play after play demonstrates that for him people are seldom what they seem. In such circumstances it is not so much legitimate as essential to treat his characters as rounded individuals. The Farmer may disappear from the scene early on (though one modern Greek production included him as a witness to subsequent events) but he affects our whole view of Elektra. Her treatment of her husband, the Chorus, Orestes and her mother consistently point to a disordered personality. This makes it psychologically sound, and I use the word without apology, that she should react as she does to the horrific reality of her mother's death. She has engineered it, claims it when Orestes backs off: 'I'll see to Mummy' (l. 647) and executes it when Orestes' nerve again fails and she has to guide the knife into Klytemnestra's body. Her subsequent collapse offers a stark contrast to the reactions of the Aeschylus and Sophocles heroines for whom Klytemnestra's death is a blessed release.

The weak-knee'd Orestes, humble Klytemnestra, blood-thirsty Old Man are rounded, believable people who may not be the everyday Athenians who will inhabit the comedies of the next century but look forward sufficiently to them to appear as fleshed-out individuals. Their quirks and failings cannot hide the human consequences of heroic deeds. Elsewhere, Euripides applies similar methods to Helen and to Herakles, to Medea and Menelaos, to a whole host of characters received from myth whose motives and actions he dissects and sabotages. This was his revenge on Aeschylus for his wooden heroes. It made him less than popular amongst audiences who were not ready for such precocious anti-heroics but it is probably one reason why more of his plays have survived than those of Aeschylus and Sophocles combined.

There is inevitably a danger in such a combative style of playwriting. The temptation for the modern reader to gild the lily and treat Euripides as a coathanger on which to hang all manner of far-fetched ideas is one that has not always been resisted by critics any more than it has been in the theatre. In the fourth century the texts had to be given a formal version, a kind of copyright, by Lycurgus, to prevent abuse. It is still a scholarly pastime to seek out and claim as late interpolation any passage that does not seem in keeping with a particular preconception. One such moment occurs in *Orestes* when a desperate Menelaos asks for the return of Helen's body from Orestes and Pylades on the palace roof. 'Pylades, are you involved in this?' asks Menelaos and it is Orestes who replies 'Of course he is. I speak for him' (ll. 1595–6). It is an odd response which some consider evidence that only three actors took part and Pylades was at that point played by a non-speaking supernumerary. In a touring company during the fourth or third century BC such a restriction may well have been necessary but it is still curious to draw attention to Pylades at this point unless some specific response is expected from him. It is unlikely that anyone will ever discover precisely what lies behind this brief exchange, though a production may discover a number of possible justifications.

The temptation is to look for a subtext in any and every line. Euripides himself chooses to parody the recognition scene from *Choephoroi* in his *Elektra*. This makes it easier to accept the uncontentious, if revolutionary, notion of a cowardly Orestes and an unappealing Elektra. But how unappealing? Obsessed with sex? Mentally unstable? Does our licence to delve extend as far as Pylades, for example, a shadowy figure who appears to have little to do and nothing to say? One possibility would be to consider him as an active personality who has persuaded Orestes to come in the first place and then sees to it that he does not renege on his commitments. There is a suggestion that he might be the messenger who brings news of Orestes' killing of Aigisthos. When the messenger first arrives Elektra demands to know who he is. 'You saw me,' he replies. 'I was with your brother' (l. 765). If this is Pylades it would account for the way in which the murder of Aigisthos is described.

Elektra's version of Aigisthos is the standard one that we might expect from Aeschylus or Sophocles. But then nothing in Euripides is predictable. Elektra claims that Aigisthos desecrates Agamemnon's grave but at the time she is keen to impress the strangers with how miserable her existence has become. The Farmer, a more reliable witness, perhaps, tells of the death sentence passed on the absent Orestes but, unlike Aeschylus and Sophocles, Euripides does not introduce Aigisthos into the action. The description of his death is superficially the completion of a necessary act of revenge. That is the language in which it is couched: the facts seem rather different. Orestes and Pylades claim to be on their way to Olympia. Aigisthos invites them to be his guests at a sacred feast. Orestes waits until Aigisthos has his hands full with a sacrificial carcass and cuts him down from behind. Necessary or not as an act of vengeance, there could hardly be a less chivalrous way to achieve it, however the account is embroidered in the telling. It is a proper prelude to the arrival of Aigisthos' body, perhaps no more than the head. For the Greeks revenge on an enemy was a legitimate ambition. Codes of behaviour were nonetheless strict. The manner in which Elektra gloats over Aigisthos transgresses all decency: as does Orestes' violation of the rules of hospitality.

If all that was implied here was a tendency to take the opposite line on almost any character from received myth, then Euripides would all too soon have become as predictable as the older style of writing he superseded. There is much more. All these subtleties of character and situation were conducted within the framework of the Greek theatre and under physical conditions that were not geared to realism in any form. The Aeschylean hero was well suited to the masked performance. Euripides, whose language is as tripping as his characters were tricky, must have found, or required to be found, an acting style which allowed physical performance to match the quickening tongue. Masked acting is comfortable with basic emotions. The language of gesture, which makes the mask a versatile performance device, heightens that performance by enhancing what is said through what is seen. It is misleading to imply that the mask hampers the actor trained in its use, or diminishes range. I have never believed this to be true and the surviving mask, or near-mask, traditions from Japan, Indonesia, India and China confirm it. The mask is as mobile for the portrayal of emotion as the actor is skilled in making it so. The Greeks used masks because that was what acting meant – putting on a mask.

What is harder to envisage is the quicksilver changes of direction that Euripides seems to demand, the subtleties and paradoxes that the previous analysis of *Elektra* seems to prescribe. Sophocles, whose own *Elektra* covers the same ground as both *Choephoroi* and the Euripides *Elektra*, chose to concentrate on the figure of Elektra herself (see Kenneth McLeish's translation in *Sophocles Plays: Two*, Methuen, 1990). His portrait of a vilified and battered victim is as revolutionary in its way as is that of Euripides. There has been a long and not always elegant scholarly argument over whether the Sophocles or the Euripides *Elektra* was presented first, so much does each appear a reaction, not only to *Choephoroi*, but to the other *Elektra*. Nothing more is proved than that all the great tragedians were quite versatile enough constantly to rerun episodes from the epic sagas. The treatment of characters was flexible enough to allow it. Whatever the dates and circumstances of the two *Elektra*s, however, there can be little disputing the way in which Sophocles writes for the masked player. This is not to suggest that his plays still need to be performed in masks. It is to indicate a different quality of writing in Euripides. Euripides is sometimes portrayed as a dramatist for whom the conventions of the theatre of his time had become irksome. Masks, chorus, the very size of the theatre restricted an imagination, it is claimed, so engaged by 'truth for truth's sake'. I would argue, if anything, that the opposite were true. Though it would have required a refined skill, the kind of subtext implied in the scenes with the Farmer, the parodied recognition scene, the deception of Klytemnestra and her murder would be well within the compass of the masked player. The stage language of the mask is most adept when it is demonstrating paradox. Why else would Brecht have returned to its use in his plays in the present century? False emotions can as easily be demonstrated through the mask as when the body language is subordinate to facial expression. That is the way that the theatre's sign system worked in the classical theatre and has done on many of the great stages of the world since.

Euripides' *Elektra*, *Orestes* and *Iphigeneia in Tauris* parade and glory in this new way to tackle realism. The subtleties are not the whim of some rationalist, though the rationalists were certainly responsible for some bizarre rationalisations about Euripides in their time. They are built into a text which is dense and complicated and which needs concentration but is, as a result, enormously rich. The modernity is in the scope offered to the contemporary actor more used to manipulating text rather than simply stating it.

The possession of three plays by different playwrights on the Elektra theme provides justification enough for concentrating so far almost exclusively on the first play in the present volume. With *Elektra* we can make a direct comparison of dramatic styles. If a comparative case can be made for Euripides asking awkward questions in *Elektra* and basing a dramatic technique on behavioural nuance, then similar methods can be applied without further argument to the other plays which treat this most familiar of family sagas.

*Orestes* might have provided as good a test case. It deals with the fate of Orestes, Pylades and Elektra in the wake of the assassination of Klytemnestra and Aigisthos. Similar ground is covered to the *Eumenides*, the third play of the *Oresteia* but, if Euripides wrote *Elektra* as a direct riposte to some popular revival of the *Oresteia*, his passion was spent by 408 BC. That is a firm date for *Orestes*, confirmed by a scholiast's note attached to a surviving manuscript which identifies the archon at the time of its performance. Not only was Euripides in his declining years but he was about to leave Athens for good. The war with Sparta was entering its final stages. The city was in turmoil and Euripides chose to pass the rest of his life in Macedon. It was there that he wrote his last plays, including *Iphigeneia at Aulis* and *Bacchae*, first performed in Athens in 405 at the Great Dionysia following his death. *Orestes* may deal with the aftermath of the murder of Klytemnestra but it is barely a comparative piece to any other play. Orestes and his sister are still in Argos but this play is set, not in the rustic landscape of the border, but in the heart of a thriving city which is about to institute the due processes of law to decide what to do with the matricides. If the Elektra of this later play is marginally preferable to the deranged slattern of *Elektra*, her brother and Pylades more than make up for that. They are to all intents and purposes a pair of killers, prepared to go to any lengths to preserve their skins. True, when the play opens Orestes is discovered asleep having suffered torments for six days since their mother's murder. But this Orestes' Furies are his conscience. The danger to his life comes from a judicial decision, not from any fledgling Areopagus, but from an Assembly curiously like that which made so many important decisions in Euripides' Athens. Orestes and Pylades have the chance to argue their case but a decision is taken to stone them to death. In the light of the way they subsequently behave it is tempting to wonder if the Assembly might not have got it right.

*Orestes* is a vicious play, filled with vicious characters, interested almost exclusively in themselves. Helen is shallow, Menelaos a backslider, Pylades, who does no more than haunt the fringes of most versions of the story, took a full part in the murder of Klytemnestra and is prime mover in the plan to kill Helen. Elektra sets up the taking of Hermione as a hostage. The only redeeming character is Tyndareus arguing that, if Orestes and Elektra had a grievance against Aigisthos and Klytemnestra, they should have invoked a perfectly good legal system. The decision of Apollo *ex machina* that he will sort everything out is the clearest evidence that Euripides' use of the device is ironic.

In the circumstances at the end of the play any denouement which is aimed at resolving the situation is likely to seem comic. And so it should. Three of the more obviously comic plays of Euripides, *Alkestis*, *Helen* and *Ion*, are included in a previous volume (*Euripides Plays: Three*, Methuen, 1997). Those are among his *pièces roses*, in the terminology by which Jean Anouilh distinguished his lighter comedies from the darker. *Orestes* and *Elektra* are decidedly *noires*, but have their comic moments. The ending of *Orestes* is prepared for by the handling of several earlier scenes. The entry of the Chorus seems as much parody as does the recognition scene in *Elektra*. The target is less Aeschylus than the whole institution of the chorus. Here is Elektra, who has just succeeded in getting her brother to sleep after six days, and a group of women arrive who insist on singing and dancing: 'Please go. Take your noise/ And leave us. Go away,' Elektra tells them. 'Please let the poor man sleep' (ll. 170–1 and 183). Finally in their concern that he may be dead, they wake him up.

More blatant comedy comes in the presentation of a frivolous Helen who has cut off a tiny lock of her hair as an offering, but from the side where it will not be noticed. The Trojan who thinks he has escaped from death in the palace only to run into Orestes at his most sadistic may consciously echo the Scythian policeman of Aristophanes' *Festival Time*

(*Aristophanes Plays: Two*, Methuen, 1993) in his inability to master the Greek language. He also serves to parody the messenger speech in his garbled account of what has happened indoors. Equally improbable is the Apollo who arrives to sort things out and blithely announces that Helen, whose death cries were earlier heard on stage, is not dead at all but has been rescued by him so she can go back home to Sparta. He promptly installs a happy ending all round by pairing off Orestes and Pylades with Hermione and Elektra. Three of the most sacred cows of Greek tragedy, chorus, messenger speech and *deus ex machina* are shown at their most absurd. Perhaps, after all, Euripides still had some bones to pick with the shade of Aeschylus.

The miraculous escape of Helen, last heard crying 'murder' in the palace, is itself an echo of the third play in the present volume, *Iphigeneia in Tauris*. Though without a firm date this is usually assumed to be from about the same time as *Helen*, first performed in 412. Against that is the remarkable similarity of *Iphigeneia in Tauris* to *Helen* in both plot and execution which might argue rather that no playwright would write two such plays in close proximity. Both *Helen* and *Iphigeneia in Tauris* offer a variant on the familiar myth. In *Helen* Euripides sets his play in Egypt where the real Helen has been wasting away for over ten years while a version fashioned out of ether was abducted by Paris and caused the Trojan War. The war now over, she encounters her husband Menelaos who has been shipwrecked and has arrived on her doorstep seeking help. After a prolonged recognition, though nothing like as prolonged as that in the *Iphigeneia in Tauris*, Helen and Menelaos plan their escape by means of a trick involving a fake sacrifice at sea for Helen's 'dead' husband. The local pharaoh, who has been trying in vain to get Helen to marry him, is left with the consolation of a divine arrival from Kastor telling him that he will have to put up with it. The play is comic in tone and offers a far more charitable portrait of Helen than that in *Orestes* or *Trojan Women*.

*Iphigeneia in Tauris* is based on a version of the story of the sacrifice of Iphigeneia at Aulis by her father Agamemnon so that the Greek army could sail to Troy to win back Helen.

Euripides' *Iphigeneia at Aulis* is the story of that sacrifice but ends with a messenger telling of a miraculous deliverance which removed Iphigeneia at the last moment and substituted a stag. Her distraught mother, Klytemnestra, believes this to be 'a lie,/ Concocted for my benefit/ To soothe me and keep me quiet' (ll. 1616–18, *Euripides Plays: Two*, Methuen, 1991). The play ends on a question mark.

*Iphigeneia at Aulis* was produced posthumously, so *Iphigeneia in Tauris* was presumably written earlier, though it could seem like a companion piece. Iphigeneia was, indeed, rescued from the knife, we discover, and is now a priestess of Artemis in Thrace where her duties include killing any Greeks who happen in. Orestes and Pylades arrive, Orestes under instruction from Apollo to redeem a statue of Artemis which had fallen from the heavens and take it to Athens. Precise reasons for this odd commission have not been vouchsafed but Orestes is told it will relieve his pain in the wake of the murder of Klytemnestra. Orestes and Pylades are arrested and brought before Iphigeneia but they are all so oblique in their answers to straight questions that only the identity of Pylades is revealed. Iphigeneia has been so long in Thrace that she knows nothing of the deaths of Klytemnestra and Aigisthos. A dream has convinced her that Orestes must be dead, hence the device of the letter, as a result of which brother and sister are finally united after three hundred lines of avoiding telling one another who they are.

Thoas, king of Thrace, must then be tricked into allowing the three of them to escape. In *Helen*, Helen persuaded Theoklymenos that she had to go to sea to perform burial rites for her dead husband. Iphigeneia tells Thoas a similar story though she has to get her hands on the statue as well. She informs Thoas that the Greeks are murderers and unfit for sacrifice. The statue has said so by wobbling and shutting its eyes at the sight of them. She must take it out to sea for purification. The convenient thing about being appointed a priestess is that you can invent all manner of mumbo-jumbo to justify yourself. Thoas is not completely gullible but accedes to all Iphigeneia's demands and the three of them make their escape. Thoas is as angry at the loss of his prisoners, his priestess and his statue as was Theoklymenos who lost his would-be bride and her husband, and nearly his sister. Athene calms Thoas down, arriving *ex machina*, and he eventually agrees to send home the chorus of Greek women anyway.

*Iphigeneia in Tauris* comes as something of a relief after *Elektra* and *Orestes*. It is another *pièce rose* in which it is difficult not to feel that everyone in the play is trying to behave with the best of motives. Thoas is more pussy-cat than ogre. Orestes suggests killing him to help their escape. Elektra will not hear of it: 'I owe him everything,' she expostulates. Orestes is far more agreeable than his counterpart elsewhere. He and Pylades are falling over one another to do the decent thing when it seems possible for only one of them to escape and relay the letter back home. Iphigeneia has been a reluctant assassin but so innocuous is the whole situation, despite the gruesome trappings, that her current job of killing Greeks seems hardly more arduous than putting out the dustbin. This is Euripides in one of his least bilious moods, rehabilitating the murderous and demented siblings of *Elektra* and *Orestes* and awarding them the kind of operetta status of Offenbach's *La Belle Hélène* or his own *Helen*.

Euripides' other Iphigeneia play, *Iphigeneia at Aulis*, was used by Ariane Mnouchkine to precede her production of *Les Atrides* (the *Oresteia*) and justify Klytemnestra's hatred of Agamemnon. Euripides sat uncomfortably alongside Aeschylus. The approach of the two playwrights is, as we have seen, one of contrast rather than similarity. *Iphigeneia at Aulis* may be a more conventionally 'tragic' piece than *Iphigeneia in Tauris* but, arguably, *Iphigeneia at Aulis* is also a tragedy, less of malice, than of good intentions, with the rescue of Iphigeneia a more suitable ending than some critics have deemed it.

Euripides' approach was idiosyncratic, but that is not to say that other playwrights were not equally innovative. The range of subjects and characters was finite. Treatment, inevitably, was original. Aeschylus and Sophocles duplicated titles, *Ixion*, *Mysians*, *Palamedes*, *Philoctetes*: but Euripides wrote a play too with each of those titles. Most of these plays have disappeared without trace, but an essay written by Dio Chrysostom in the first century AD compares the approach of the three playwrights to *Philoctetes*. This is a particularly intriguing document because the Sophocles *Philoctetes* is one of the seven of his that we have (see *Sophocles Plays: Two*, Methuen, 1991).

Novelty was essential. Euripides used the theatre to challenge attitudes that many of his countrymen took for granted. In a time of war he challenged the reasons for continuing it, stressing its miseries rather than its glories. In a civilisation which took for granted the supremacy of the citizen male, he created female characters whose wretchedness was the result of male behaviour. He debunked heroes, and rehabilitated villains. His Oresteses and Elektras had to be different from those of other playwrights. Equally they had to be different from any other of his own creations with the same name. Any of the plays may be linked in performance and a modern director may choose what links will suit. Here is a versatility that few, if any, subsequent playwrights have been able to rival.

J. Michael Walton
University of Hull, 1997

*Transliteration from Greek into English presents problems of consistency. The names of the playwrights are more familiar as Aeschylus, Sophocles and Menander than as Aischulos, Sophokles and Menandros. Otherwise direct transliteration has normally been adopted.*

*Line numbers alongside the text refer to the Greek original rather than the English translations.*

# TRANSLATOR'S INTRODUCTION

## Euripides and the Orestes myth

Euripides seems to have been fascinated by the myth-cycle surrounding the Trojan War and its aftermath. Something like one third of all his plays, including almost half of those which survive, dealt with people (Palamedes, Rhesos, Telephos) who were involved in the war, or describe what happened afterwards to such characters as Hecuba, Andromache and Helen. Four surviving plays deal with the royal dynasty of Argos: the Greek supreme commander Agamemnon, his murderous wife Klytemnestra and their children Iphigeneia, Elektra and Orestes. (Chrysothemis, the fourth child who features in Sophocles' *Elektra*, does not appear.)

The four plays were all composed separately, and were not designed as a single unit, in the manner of Aeschylus' trilogy *Oresteia*. None the less, they were written in the same creative period, a dozen years at the end of Euripides' life: *Elektra* appeared in about 414 BC, *Iphigeneia in Tauris* some five years later, *Orestes* four years after that, and *Iphigeneia at Aulis* posthumously in 405 BC. Of the four, *Iphigeneia at Aulis* stands apart from the others. It deals not with events after the war but with its prelude, Agamemnon's sacrifice of Iphigeneia at Aulis. It stands in the same kind of relationship to the Oresteian plays as Wagner's *Rhinegold* does to the rest of his *Ring*: it uses similar themes and refers to events from a similar point of view, but has a different tone and 'speed' from the others, is self-standing while they form a conceptual unity. Although *Elektra*, *Orestes* and *Iphigeneia in Tauris* are separate, independent plays, taken together they elaborate themes, explore areas of experience and develop points of style in ways which elevate the whole experience into far more than merely the sum of its parts.

The three plays start from the same point as other surviving works on the family of Agamemnon, Aeschylus' *Oresteia* and Sophocles' *Elektra*. That is, they are concerned with the effects on Agamemnon and his family of his disastrous involvement with the gods at Aulis. Here, like Abraham in the

Bible Old Testament, he was ordered to show his trust in God by killing his own child. But where Abraham was innocent and pious (and was rewarded when an angel rescued Isaac from the knife and substituted a ram), Agamemnon was labouring both under a dynastic curse and from an offence of his own against Artemis, killing her sacred deer. God (Artemis) rescued Iphigeneia from sacrifice and substituted a fawn, but instead of doing so openly (as in the story of Abraham and Isaac), she stole the child miraculously away to the ends of the earth, and let Agamemnon, his family and the other Greeks believe that he had killed her with his own hand.

The surviving plays, by all three tragedians, show how these long-past events affected the remaining members of the family. All agree that Agamemnon's wife Klytemnestra used the supposed murder of Iphigeneia to justify her own behaviour: taking a lover (Aigisthos), banishing Orestes, humiliating Elektra and murdering Agamemnon when he returned from Troy. The point is clearly made that she had private, personal and political reasons for what she did, and understood nothing of the deeper workings of the family curse. (Her misconception about what happened at Aulis is typical of the way mortals, in Greek tragedies of the more schematic kind, fail to see the truth of what concerns the gods.) From the moment of Agamemnon's murder onwards, however, Euripides diverges from both Aeschylus and Sophocles. Each of them drives the story forward to a definite conclusion, as Agamemnon's children gradually understand more of the gods' purposes than their mother or father ever did. Sophocles is interested in purgation – not the effect on audience emotion claimed for tragedy by Aristotle, but, more directly and more doctrinally, how one person can expiate another's sin, how a chain of hatred and revenge can be ended and the gods' purposes fulfilled. Elektra and Orestes earn happiness by inherent innocence purified in the fires of enormous suffering, and their killing of Klytemnestra and Aigisthos is a catharsis, a philosophical and ethical rite of passage towards that happiness. Aeschylus goes further, setting the murders and the expiation of one family's guilt in a wider context of the nature of universal justice and civic responsibility; in his scheme of things evolution of understanding happens not just to human beings but to the supernatural powers themselves.

Euripides, writing a generation later, for fellow-citizens whose sense of personal and social identity had been affected both by the catastrophic events of nearly two decades of the Peloponnesian War and by the huge increase of religious, ethical and social questioning which it fostered, takes a different line from either of his colleagues. He is not interested in answers, in certainties, but in questions. What happens if the supernatural powers do not evolve and develop (as in Aeschylus), but remain exactly the same however much our human perception of the divine is changed by events? What if murdering Klytemnestra and Aigisthos has none of the hoped-for purgative effect, but produces no benefit, either socially or in the murderers' souls? And crucially, how should human beings cope with, and find happiness in, a chaotic and anarchic universe in which the gods are at best indifferent to humans and at the worst devious and malign?

Euripides never answers such questions. Instead of gradually narrowing the argument (as his contemporary Socrates might have done) from a wide general picture to a close-focused conclusion, he presents his ideas prismatically, examining them from different angles, picking them up and discarding them like a child with toys, consistently avoiding progression and resolution. The plays bustle with action, are crammed with reflection and argument – and the whole point is that none of it leads the characters anywhere. Each dilemma faced, each problem 'solved', merely opens the way to new ideas and confrontations, previously unforeseen. The characters deal always and only with the moment; they have no conception of wider purposes or meanings in what they do – and every time human affairs boil up to some point of unavoidable explosion, the gods appear out of nowhere, sort things out like parents arbitrating a children's quarrel ('You go there; you do that; you be nice to her') – and produce an effect not of forward movement but of return to the continuum, of resolution which is no resolution, something as arbitrary (and potentially as lethal) as the situations which led the characters to bursting-point in the first place.

The bleakness of these *deus ex machina* appearances is

matched by Euripides' savage parody, several times in these plays, of Orestes' trial and the calming of the Furies from Aeschylus' *Eumenides* (events to which the whole *Oresteia* leads), and by the anguished questioning which Orestes directs at the gods in general and his patron Apollo in particular. In Euripides' scheme of things, only Iphigeneia seems satisfied with her divine mistress – and the irony, made perfectly explicit, is that that mistress (Artemis) is an enigmatic combination of bloodthirstiness and motherly warmth, and that carrying her (in the person of her statue) from the ends of the earth to Athens will neither soften nor control her nature. The burial-ritual proposed for Iphigeneia – she will be wrapped in the silk dresses left in the shrine on behalf of mothers dead in childbirth (*Iphigeneia*, ll. 1460ff.) – may be less bloodthirsty than Artemis' constant demand for human sacrifice in Tauris – a reflection of her thirst for Iphigeneia's own blood at Aulis all those years before – but it is hardly less archaic or bizarre.

In modern terms, Euripides' dislocations and ironies are an alienation technique which reaches out to the spectators, forcing us to think about the issues. A collection of images, of instances, is presented, and if moral and philosophical coherence is to be found, it is up to us to find it. The style of the plays shows a similar take-it-or-leave-it, entirely deliberate anarchy. High-flown poetry, parody, lyrics, jokes, rhetoric, sententious moral-drawing, music and dance – Euripides dips in and takes handfuls, as if from a bran-tub, and if there are disjunctions and contradictions, he ignores them. One of his chief ironical devices is to show, at moments of enormous individual tension or crisis, how silly and panicky people can be, and how, instead of using grand phrases to articulate sublime reactions and intentions (as one might, perhaps, expect in 'tragedy'), they mumble, turn to cliché, make puns or sometimes refuse to say anything coherent at all. If Orestes, in Aeschylus, is a prototype Hamlet, in Euripides he is an arrogant adolescent facing problems which are far too deep for him. Elektra, in the midst of her self-lacerating refusal to compromise with her lust for revenge, fusses and frets about the niceties of social etiquette. Every 'high' character is obsessed, and self-obsessed; only the 'low' characters show any glimmer of wider understanding or sympathy, and the gods, highest characters of all, are also the most frivolous and vacuous.

Euripides dazzlingly sustains the effect of arbitrariness. A recognition scene is undercut even as it happens – and then it happens anyway (*Elektra*, ll. 520–80). Faced with coping with the Furies, three characters devise a ludicrous murder like the Famous Five arranging a picnic (*Orestes*, ll. 1101–30), and then switch, in the blink of a single line (l. 1189), to kidnapping. The Chorus give a learned exposition of one of the most obscure corners of the background myth – and then tell us it's just a story, means nothing at all (*Elektra*, ll. 699ff.). People suddenly start singing, while others go on talking (*Iphigeneia*, ll. 642ff.). Delivery of a letter is built up, as if it were the most important event in the universe – and then happens, matter-of-factly, in half a line (*Iphigeneia*, l. 790). The characters think about only one thing at a time, running obsessively along like toy trains; when they come to a junction they change direction and rush in an entirely new direction, as frantically as before – and the style and language switch just as singlemindedly and just as randomly.

Euripides' sleight of hand is to make all this both engrossing and intellectually engaging, and he does it not with the grand manner of an Aeschylus or with prim Sophoclean logic, but by splatter-gunning us with brilliance, leaping from effect to effect like a demented conjurer. He neither seduces his audience nor allows them to surrender: he is an intellectual terrorist, tossing bomb after bomb to keep us on our toes.

## Translating Euripides

Euripides' theatre-texts are entirely different from those of his great contemporaries. Aeschylus' plays are sonorous poetry, in which the 'musical' fall of the lines and the opulence of the text are major parts of the effect. Sophocles sets terrible events and piercing ironies against a linguistic dance as precise and neat as (say) Racine's: dislocation between what is being said and the manner of saying it is the nature of the experience. In both writers, syntax is complex and ornate, and the Chorus gives an ever-present weight, a kind of immanence, to the action, controlling (or at least strongly influencing) forward movement and the deployment of dramatic time.

Euripides' style, by contrast, is light, suggestive, floating and self-conscious – in plain terms, 'experimental'. Most of the choruses are urgent, fragmented, elliptical and (to modern ears) almost evasive in the way they set up resonances and establish or change moods without ever settling down to explore them. The dialogue is in loose, resolved metres, closer to Greek comedy, or to such formalised prose as Plato's, than to the granite lines of Aeschylus or Sophocles. It shows us the characters' minds working, flickering from one idea, one mood, to another, blurting things out. It is impressionistic: dabs and jets of ideas, real conversation trapped on the page. Long speeches tend to start with rhetorical formality, before the ideas run away with the characters and the formal house of cards collapses. There are ironies and direction-changes within each phrase or sentence; you can almost feel the characters straining to articulate their feelings, to reveal the truth of themselves or their situation in words.

All this poses problems for the translator – problems which translators in the past, rather grandly, ignored altogether. Many came from the study or teaching-room rather than the theatre; they had expert knowledge of syntax and grammar, but little idea of how actors use the 'space' and 'air' in a line, how the less you give them the more they give you back. For an audience which more often read the plays than saw them performed, they produced literary texts, and the result was that their Euripides tended to seem like a diluted version of Aeschylus or Sophocles, a poet of putty rather than marble. The 'faults' in the plays which this practice seemed to reveal were blamed on inadequate technique on Euripides' part – 'X is not a very good play' – or on bad manuscripts – 'lines must be missing here' or 'this gibberish is the fault of some illiterate copyist' – or even on actors' interpolations. Ordinary literary and dramatic criticism, such as was applied to other stage writers in the Western tradition, was not a common weapon in the Classical scholarly armoury, and the result was that plays like *Medea* were claimed as flawed masterpieces (because Sophocles would have treated the situations 'better'), plays like *Elektra* were compared (to their detriment) with work on similar subjects by other writers, and plays like *Iphigeneia in Tauris* were dismissed out of hand as 'romances' or 'tragi-comedies' equipped with that most un-Aristotelian procedure, a happy ending.

There was a huge upsurge of this kind of thing in the 1900s–1930s, when Gilbert Murray's translations were not only published but performed, and many Euripides plays first reached the English-speaking stage. Except that they were not Euripides' plays, but Murray's. Murray was a genius at classical texts, not at living English or living theatre – and his vision of how Euripides 'went' affected later translators right down to several of those whose works are still widely available and widely read.

In the last thirty years of the twentieth century, things began to change. Beginning with David Thompson in the 1970s, directors and actors began to explore Euripides afresh, to mine him for his own personal qualities inherent in the texts, rather than his adherence to or departure from some pre-established critical tradition. And the result was a revelation. It was as if we had known nothing of Western music except the classics – Brahms, Mahler, Haydn, Schubert – and suddenly discovered not only that jazz existed, but that it had important things to say and unique ways of saying them. Euripides' fragmented, edgy style and his concentration on 'odd' corners and details of the original stories released actors to explore the psychological and philosophical ideas underlying the drama, and to develop their own performances, in ways we were more used to in Pinter or Beckett than in Athenian tragedy. Euripides provides magnificent opportunities for that self-investigatory, inner-journey style of acting so much the norm today: his parts are built outwards from a central core, as a sculptor makes a clay figure, rather than chiselled from an existing block of stone.

The implications for translators are obvious. It is possible still to write 'literary' versions of Euripides' Greek – and some are excellent. But the heart of the experience lies elsewhere, and in particular depends on trying to match every breathless turn and swoop, every tiny sunshaft of language, every banality, pun or syntactical twist. There is not one possibility for every word, phrase or speech – there are dozens, and you should leave your text as open, as accessible to directors and actors, as possible. Often, I find, when 'strangenesses' occur, it is best not to interpret them and smoothe them out, but to leave them as they stand.

A specific example makes the point. Euripides' Greek is full of exclamations – 'feoo', 'oee moee', and so on. Each occurs in precise situations, and seems to articulate a distinct emotional mood. Previous translations omitted them, or replaced them with anodyne English phrases like 'Alas!' or 'Oh woe!'. I have transliterated but not interpreted them. I think that they may not have been intended to be spoken or sung exactly; rather, each gave the actor the cue for a vocal melisma or cadenza, spoken or sung; emotion distilled not into words but into pure sound. In the mid-1990s, research by Thanos Vovolis suggested that in the ancient theatre each sound may have resonated in the mask in a highly individual way. In workshops, modern actors have used them in all kinds of ways, from inhalations of breath to improvised cries. Or they can be omitted: the choice is the performer's. (In lines 1368–1535 of *Orestes*, Euripides goes further, giving the Trojan slave occasional words which are half Greek, half gibberish. They must have sounded as bizarre to his audience as they do to us, and I have, again, not translated but merely transliterated them.)

Kenneth McLeish, 1997

*The choruses are written in* strophe *and* antistrophe *style. Each* strophe – *the word means 'turn', a reference to choreography not content* – *is a group of lines united in theme or rhythm and matched by an answering* antistrophe. *In some plays, without disturbing the* strophe/antistrophe *groupings, the choruses are further divided into individual voices, expressing particular points of view or a sudden quickening of rhythm. These changes are indicated by dashes, one for each change of speaker.*

This trio of translations was commissioned by the Gate Theatre, London, and was first performed there in February 1995. The plays were presented separately, and also as a composite experience ('Agamemnon's Children'), all three on a single day. The cast, in alphabetical order, was as follows:

| | |
|---|---|
| ATHENE/CHORUS | Uche Aniagola |
| CHORUS LEADER (*Orestes*)/CHORUS | Sherry Baines |
| CHORUS LEADER (*Iphigeneia*)/CHORUS | Yasmin Bannerman |
| ORESTES | Charles Daish |
| IPHIGENEIA | Barbara Flynn |
| OLD MAN/POLYDEUKES/ TYNDAREOS/ATTENDANT | Patrick Godfrey |
| CHORUS LEADER (*Elektra*)/CHORUS | Caroline Lennon |
| SERVANT OF ORESTES/TROJAN | Kevork Malikyan |
| ELEKTRA/CHORUS | Sara Mair Thomas |
| HERMIONE/CHORUS | Poppy Miller |
| KLYTEMNESTRA/CHORUS | Etela Pardo |
| FARMER/KASTOR/MENELAOS/ HERDSMAN | Ian Redford |
| PYLADES | Velibor Topic |
| CHORUS DRUMMER | Jayne Trotman |
| HELEN/CHORUS | Thalia Valeta |

*Director* Laurence Boswell
*Designer* Anthony McIlwaine
*Costume Designer* Sammy Haworth
*Lighting Designer* Jenny Kagan
*Music* Mick Sands
*Movement* Christian Flint

# ELEKTRA

*translated by Kenneth McLeish*

# Characters

FARMER
ELEKTRA
ORESTES
PYLADES★
OLD MAN
KLYTEMNESTRA
KASTOR
POLYDEUKES (non-speaking)
CHORUS OF WOMEN
ATTENDANTS (non-speaking)

★*Translator's note*: In the original, Pylades doesn't speak: the
account of Aigisthos' death is given by a Servant

*Outside the* FARMER's *cottage. Just before dawn. Enter*
FARMER.

FARMER.
   This is Argos, glory of Greece.
   From here, these streams, this plain,
   Lord Agamemnon sailed for Troy.
   He killed the Trojan king, sacked Troy,
   That city of ancient kings, sailed home again
   And piled our temples high with Trojan gold,
   The splendour of the East.
   So far so good. But then he died.
   Murdered. Klytemnestra his wife
   And Aigisthos her bedmate murdered him.         10
   The king was dead, long live the king:
   Aigisthos, Klytemnestra his consort.
   There were also two children,
   Agamemnon's children,
   Left when he sailed to Troy: his son, Orestes,
   Elektra, his daughter, young children still.
   Aigisthos planned to kill Orestes
   (The son and heir), but an old man,
   Agamemnon's old servant,
   Who loved Orestes, loved him like a father,
   Stole him away to Phokis, where he grew up
   In the care of King Strophios, safe and sound.

   Agamemnon's daughter, on the other hand,
   Elektra: she stayed, she grew up,               20
   Young bachelors swarmed round
   From every state in Greece. Princes, suitors –
   A problem. Suppose she had a son,
   And the son grew up to avenge
   The death of his grandfather Agamemnon?
   No marriage, Aigisthos decreed;
   She was to stay at home. Then he thought again.
   She didn't need to marry to bear a son;
   Better kill her. Klytemnestra then,
   Flint-hearted mother though she was, intervened,
   Saved her. She'd had cause enough

To kill Agamemnon, she reasoned,
30   But none at all to murder her daughter
And revolt all Greece. Aigisthos thought again.
He made a proclamation: a fortune in gold
To anyone who executed Orestes, the exile.
And as for Elektra, he married her to me:
Not nobody, you understand – good honest stock,
I'm proud of them – but not really anybody either.
Lack of cash: a good family, fallen on hard times:
'No risk from him,' Aigisthos must have thought.
40   'No stirring up old memories, no punishment to pay
For murdering Agamemnon all those years ago.'
Well, I married her. But I swear,
Aphrodite hear me, I've kept away from her,
She's slept alone. Still virgin.
She *is* a princess, I mean it's not for me to . . .
Not my place. It's Orestes I'm thinking of,
My brother-in-law, at least in name –
I want him to come home one day
And find no shame on his sister
Because of this marriage.
50   What? I'm an idiot? A beautiful young girl,
A virgin bride, and I don't take advantage?
You've dirty minds. No question, dirty minds.

*Enter* ELEKTRA.

ELEKTRA.
Night! Darkness! Nurse of golden stars,
Look down on me. I'm going to the spring,
For water. There's no need for it:
I choose to do it, choose to let all Heaven see
What Aigisthos does to me, choose to fill the sky
With tears for Agamemnon my father.
60   As for her, that she-wolf, mother no-mother,
She bears Aigisthos' brats, humiliates us,
Orestes, Elektra, turns us out, makes us nothing –

FARMER.
Elektra, why are you doing this, humiliating
    yourself?
There's no need for this. You weren't born for it.

Why don't you listen? I keep on telling you.

ELEKTRA.
How kind you are, a god:
The way you treat me,
Take no advantage.
A friend in need – what greater joy,
Greater cure for the misery of life?                    70
I know you don't ask it,
But I must share the chores,
Must help you, play my part.
You've enough to do in the fields;
Inside, it's up to me. When a working man
Comes home after a hard day's toil
He's a right to find everything just as it should be.

FARMER.
All right, this once.
The well's over there: not far.
As soon as it's light I'll harness the oxen,
Get on with the harrowing.
Fine words butter no parsnips,                          80
It's honest toil that makes an honest penny . . .

*Exeunt. Enter* ORESTES *and* PYLADES.

ORESTES.
Pylades, dear friend, Orestes' only friend,
In everything that's happened you've stood by me
Since Aigisthos did . . . what he did to me,
Since he killed my father. Aigisthos – and her,
Blood-mother. No one knows we're here.
Apollo sent us: we're to take revenge,
Wreak vengeance, kill the killers.
We came in the night. We went to Father's grave,    90
I wept, left a lock of hair,
Sacrificed a lamb, and no one heard.
Their Majesties don't know we're here,
Don't know we're in Argos.
This is border-country, far out of town.
If anyone sees us, we slip across,
Slip out of sight. My sister's here, they say:

She's married, grown up, lives here.
She'll tell me how everything stands in Argos.
100 She'll hear my plans, to murder them, and help.
It's dawn; light soon.
Stand back from the path.
We'll wait and ask –
A labourer, perhaps,
Or a slave-girl –
They'll know where Elektra lives.
Someone's coming.
A slave: shorn hair, water-pot.
Keep down!
110 We'll listen to what she says:
She may tell us, without seeing us,
What we want to know.

*They hide. Music. Enter* ELEKTRA *from the well.*

ELEKTRA.
Hurry. It's late.
Weep. Walk. Weep.
Eeoh moee moee.
Agamemnon's daughter:
Her daughter,
Bitch-mother,
Klytemnestra.
How can I bear it?
Elektra, poor Elektra they call me,
120 Feoo feoo, misery, despair.
O Father, deep in death you lie.
They did it: they cut you down,
Your wife no-wife, her bedmate.

Weep with me.
Find tears for me,
Gorge on it, oh weep.

Hurry. It's late.
Weep. Walk. Weep.
Eeoh moee moee.
Orestes! Brother of grief,
Where are you?

What city, what exile,
Where, oh where?                                   130
They stole you away,
I wept for you, wept.
Feoo feoo,
Our father's murder,
They did it, I spit on them,
Spit on them.
Orestes, home,
Blood for blood,
Come home.

Put it down,
Put the water down.                                140
Now weep, weep now.
Sun rising.
Gorge on grief,
Sing songs of death,
For my father, dead.
Where are you sleeping, Father?
In darkness, darkness.
Shame the sky with tears.
Tear cheeks, beat head, beat breast.
Aee aee. He's gone.
Weep for him, sing:                                150
A swan, there by the lake,
Weeping, calling,
Its father dead, netted.
O Agamemnon, Father,
They netted you, snared you,
I weep for you.

We laid you out, washed you,
Made you neat for death.
Eeoh moee, eeoh moee.
They cut you, cut you:
Home from Troy you came,
They took a net, an axe,
They chopped. She laughed,                          160
Wore crowns of flowers
To welcome you, enticed you

There where her bedmate was waiting:
Aigisthos, axe waiting in the dark.
She smiled at him,
He chopped you down,
She laughed.

*Enter* CHORUS.

CHORUS.
Agamemnon's child,
Elektra, here in these hills,
In this empty place, we visit you.
170     A man came, a man from the city.
There's a festival, two days away.
Young girls of the city: a procession,
Singing in Hera's temple, dancing.

ELEKTRA.
I won't sing,
Won't wear fine dresses, gold,
Won't lighten my heart,
Won't dance,
180     Whirling, stamping.
I weep the hours away,
Night, day, weep time away.
Look at me:
Rags, chopped hair –
How could I dance,
Agamemnon's daughter dance,
Agamemnon who toppled Troy?

CHORUS.
For Hera's sake,
190     Elektra, for Hera's sake,
I'll lend you a dress – please let me –
A lovely dress, a necklace, gold.
What good will they do,
These tears, these cries?
Will you hurt your enemies with tears?
Dance, pray to God,
Ask God to help you.

ELEKTRA.
  Day after day
  I pray to the gods –
  They're deaf.                           200
  His blood
  Calls from this earth
  To them, day after day –
  They're deaf.
  My brother cries,
  His exile cries –
  They're deaf.
  Here in these hills
  Agamemnon's daughter withers,           210
  In the palace bitch-mother beds it,
  Beds it in blood.

  *Music ends.*

CHORUS.
  Helen did this, your mother's sister,
  Helen, Hell-to-Men. She ripped all Greece apart.

ELEKTRA.
  Hush now, women.
  There are men here, strangers.
  They're hiding. They'll hurt us.
  Run: that way, down the path.
  I'll run to the house.

  ORESTES *and* PYLADES *come out.*

ORESTES.
  It's all right. I won't hurt you.          220

ELEKTRA.
  Apollo, protect me. Save me.

ORESTES.
  I harm only enemies. You're safe.

ELEKTRA.
  Go away. Don't touch me. You've no right –

ORESTES.
  No one on earth has more right than I.

ELEKTRA.
You lurk in the bushes, you wear a sword –
How dare you?

ORESTES.
If you wait, and listen, I'll tell you.

ELEKTRA.
What else can I do? Don't hurt me.

ORESTES.
I've news of your brother.

ELEKTRA.
Oh, wonderful! Is he alive, or dead?

ORESTES.
230   The best news first: he's alive.

ELEKTRA.
God reward you for that.

ORESTES.
God reward us both.

ELEKTRA.
Where is he, poor man, poor exile?

ORESTES.
He wanders. Calls no place home.

ELEKTRA.
He's hungry?

ORESTES.
For his rights, not for gold.

ELEKTRA.
You're here because of him?

ORESTES.
I'm to see if you're alive, how things are with you.

ELEKTRA.
I'm as you see: a shadow –

ORESTES.
240   Worn with tears. I weep to see it.

ELEKTRA.
Hair shorn. Scalped.

ORESTES.
For Orestes? For your father?

ELEKTRA.
Oee moee, they're all I love.

ORESTES.
Feoo feoo.
D'you think Orestes has forgotten you?

ELEKTRA.
He stays away. He doesn't come.

ORESTES.
Why do you live out here, so far from Argos?

ELEKTRA.
They made me marry. They destroyed me.

ORESTES.
And I was weeping for Orestes. A man of rank?

ELEKTRA.
Not the one Agamemnon chose for me.

ORESTES.
Tell me: your brother will want to know.                250

ELEKTRA.
This is where we live.

ORESTES.
What is he? A cowherd? A labourer?

ELEKTRA.
He's kind: poor but generous.

ORESTES.
Generous? In what way, generous?

ELEKTRA.
We sleep in separate beds. He's never –

ORESTES.
Doesn't he like you? Has he sworn some vow?

ELEKTRA.
He respects my rank.

ORESTES.
Such a glittering marriage! He must hug himself.

ELEKTRA.
He knows it was forced on me –

ORESTES.
260 And he's frightened of Orestes –

ELEKTRA.
Perhaps. But he's a good man too, an honest man.

ORESTES.
H'm, honest. He'll need rewarding.

ELEKTRA.
Yes, if Orestes ever comes.

ORESTES.
Didn't your mother try to stop this?

ELEKTRA.
Women go with their lovers, not their children.

ORESTES.
Aigisthos did this, smeared you. Why?

ELEKTRA.
In case I bore royal princes –

ORESTES.
Who might demand revenge?

ELEKTRA.
God destroy him, yes.

ORESTES.
270 He knows you're still a virgin?

ELEKTRA.
We've never told him.

ORESTES.
Can you trust these women, listening?

ELEKTRA.
Whatever we say, they'll keep it to themselves.

ORESTES.
Then: what could Orestes do, if he came back home?

ELEKTRA.
If? Could? You insult him.
He can! He must!

ORESTES.
You mean, kill the killers,
His father's killers. How?

ELEKTRA.
Without a pang of mercy —
They killed, they die.

ORESTES.
But your mother —
Would you help him kill your mother?

ELEKTRA.
I'd use the axe she used. I'd lift it and laugh.

ORESTES.
I can tell him that? You mean it?                    280

ELEKTRA.
I'll see her blood spurting, and die content.

ORESTES.
Feoo. If only he were here —

ELEKTRA.
I wouldn't know him if I saw him.

ORESTES.
Of course not. You were children, both of you.

ELEKTRA.
There's only one person I trust,
Who'd know him now.

ORESTES.
The man who saved him, rescued him?

ELEKTRA.
My father's old servant. Long retired.

ORESTES.
Tell me about Agamemnon's grave.

ELEKTRA.
> It's nothing special.
> They carried him out and dumped him.

ORESTES.
290
> Oee moee . . . I'm sorry. I'm a stranger,
> Naturally, but still I understand.
> Fellow-feeling: I'm not a stone, I suffer.
> Tell me everything, however unsavoury.
> Your brother wants to know.

CHORUS.
> We'd also like to hear.
> – We didn't live near.
> – We'd like to hear.

ELEKTRA.
300
> All right. Fellow-feeling:
> You say you understand.
> What happened to my father, to me: I'll tell you.
> I'm ashamed, tell Orestes that, ashamed –
> Of the way they've treated us,
> Of the clothes I wear,
> Of the poverty here, this . . . palace . . . I live in.
> I make my own clothes: it's that or go naked.
> I fetch water, with my own hands: look.
310
> No feasts on holy days, no dancing – I'm a virgin,
> How do I know what married women think,
> How can I talk to them? I was to marry Kastor,
> Prince Kastor of Sparta, the one who became a god.
> He courted me, now he's gone –
> And there my mother sits, on a golden throne,
> In dresses of royal silk,
> With a gaggle of waiting-women, the spoils of Troy,
> My father's spoils, pretty frocks, gold bangles,
> And over it all the stench of my father's blood,
> Black blood, oozing, festering. The killer's there,
320
> Showing off in Father's chariot, blood-hands
> Swinging Father's sceptre, that ruled all Greece.
> Agamemnon's grave, you ask about that?
> I'll tell you. No offerings, no sacrifice,
> No funeral wreaths. His Highness,

Mother's bedmate, fills himself with drink,
Jumps over it, throws stones at the headstone.
'Agamemnon – ha! And Orestes – ha!
Where is he? Why isn't he here?
Is that all he thinks of you?                                    330
Look how he leaves your grave!'

That's what it's like. Tell Orestes. Please.
We cry for him, all of us, we cry for him:
These hands, this face, this heart,
This head, cropped head –
And Father cries, his father,
Agamemnon who toppled Troy.
Orestes is young, he's strong,
He's Agamemnon's son –
We don't want a city toppling,
We want him to kill one man.

CHORUS.
Excuse me, Elektra. Your husband's coming.
He's noticed the strangers. He's hurrying.                      340

   *Enter* FARMER.

FARMER.
You. Who are you? Strangers.
What d'you want? This is my farm –
Are you looking for me? Inside, woman:
You shouldn't be out here, talking to strangers.

ELEKTRA.
It's all right. These gentlemen have news,
News of Orestes.
(*To* ORESTES *and* PYLADES.) I do apologise . . .

FARMER.
What is their news? He's alive?

ELEKTRA.
So they say – and they seem to know.                            350

FARMER.
Know – what's happened to you, to Agamemnon?

ELEKTRA.
What can Orestes do?

He's an exile. He has no resources.

FARMER.
He sent these gentlemen?

ELEKTRA.
To see how I am, how I suffer.

FARMER.
And what they haven't seen, you've told them.

ELEKTRA.
What there is to know, they know.

FARMER.
Then why haven't you asked them in?
Gentlemen, come inside. You're welcome:
A poor cottage, but all it has is yours.
360   The slaves will bring your bags. Say yes.
Please: Orestes' friends – you're welcome.
I may not have much, but in loyalty I'm rich.

ORESTES.
Elektra, is that the man you married
To save your honour, Orestes' honour?

ELEKTRA.
That's the man:
Elektra's husband, princess of tears.

ORESTES.
Feoo.
It just goes to show, we should never judge
Other people by what they look like.
Character matters more than appearance.
Kings' sons can be worthless,
370   Moral pigmies can breed giants,
A coward wear silks and satins, a hero rags.
Then how are we to judge?
By wealth, position? No.
By poverty? Just as risky:
Lack of means often spurs people on to crime.
Behaviour in battle?
That's impossible to judge: you're so busy
Avoiding your enemies' swords and spears

You've no time to study
How well your neighbour's doing.
Take as you find, perhaps that's the best way.
This man, for example:
He's nobody, a man in the street,                            380
And when need arises
Look what a prince he is.
There's a lesson here for us all:
Stop philosophising,
Making maps and charts of virtue;
Start with a clean slate with everyone you meet,
See what they do and what they say, then judge.
But be careful. There are posers in public life,
Flaunting their looks, their brawn, their readiness –
And then, when the struggle comes,
Pricked balloons, show without substance,
No inner strength . . .                                       390

However,
Agamemnon's son Orestes, for whom I stand,
Accepts this fellow's welcome. We'll go inside.
He has nothing, but he offers us all he has.
We accept his welcome, gladly. As easily as this
May Orestes your brother one day step inside
His own high hall, his power and wealth restored.
He will: God said he would, Apollo –
And unlike human prophets, God never lies.            400

   *He and* PYLADES *go in.*

CHORUS.
   Elektra, it's happening.
   – Things are on the mend.
   – Bad times are over.
   – Soon misery will end.

ELEKTRA (*to the* FARMER).
   What are you playing at,
   Asking them in like that?
   They're men of rank:
   There's nothing in there for them.

FARMER.
   If they're what they seem to be, they'll fit.

ELEKTRA.
   Fit! Fool! Go and find that old man,
410   Agamemnon's old servant. By the river,
   A shepherd since they threw him out of Argos.
   Tell him Elektra has guests,
   She needs provisions, now,
   Something worthwhile to offer them.
   He'll be on his knees with joy
   When he hears about Orestes,
   The child he saved. Go on.
   We'll get nothing from her, my mother –
   Nothing but death, if she hears Orestes lives.

FARMER.
   All right, I'll find him, tell him.
420   You go inside, do the best you can.
   A woman always manages –
   Whatever scraps there are,
   Conjures up a feast.
   And if you can't,
   If they have to go hungry,
   It hardly matters, for just one day.
   I always say, 'If you've got it, spend it –
   Food for visitors, doctors' bills –
430   And if you haven't, put up with it.'
   It's not as if rich people's bellies
   Are bigger than anyone else's . . .

   *Exit.*

CHORUS.
   Ships of Greece,
   Butting sea for Troy,
   Dancing, oars dancing,
   Sea-nymphs dancing,
   Dolphins leaping,
   Your dark beaks butting,
   Butting sea for Troy;
   Achilles leaping,

Agamemnon,                                            440
Skimming sea for Troy.

Down they came,
Nymphs of the mountains,
In their arms armour,
Golden armour,
Prince's armour,
Achilles' armour,
Forged for him by God.
Down, mountain-nymphs, down,
Armour for Achilles,                                  450
Fire of hope for Greece.

God forged it, Achilles,
Your sun and moon,
Your shield to dazzle Troy.
Monster-slayers
God carved on it:
Perseus,
In his hands the Gorgon's head                        460
Whose glance turns flesh to stone,
And beside him Hermes,
Hovering, winged sandals,
Messenger of God.

At its heart glowing,
A wheel of fire, the sun;
Winged horses, stars, dancing,
Storm-bringers, despair for Troy.
Golden helmet, sphinxes pouncing,                     470
Riddling, sharp death for Troy.
The Trojan lion snorts fire, turns,
Runs, runs from the hunt,
Winged horses, Greek.

Achilles' sword,
A chariot team, four horses,
Galloping, dust-clouds,
Soldiers, numberless –
See, Klytemnestra, see!                               480
Agamemnon led them, your husband,

The warlord you sent to death.
God saw, God hunts you down.
Adultery! You'll pay,
White throat, sharp knife, blood, death –
It's coming, we'll see it, see it.

*Music ends. Enter* OLD MAN.

OLD MAN.
Where is she? Elektra? My princess, my dear?
My princess, his baby, Agamemnon's baby,
My Agamemnon's baby? I'm too old for this:
490    Steep path, bad back, this knee.
Don't give up now.
There's your darling, your princess,
Don't give up now.

Elektra, there you are.
Here, child, look, a lamb:
Newborn, from my own flock.
And here, look, cheeses; flowers;
Something from the cellar,
Not big, but old, full-bodied –
Such a bouquet! – good for mixing.
Get someone to take them in,
500    Serve them to your visitors.
I'm sorry, I can't help it,
Old eyes, just let me wipe my eyes.

ELEKTRA.
Uncle, what's wrong?
Is it for me you're weeping?
For Orestes, so long away?
For Father,
The prince you brought up for this, for this?

OLD MAN.
As I was coming here, I passed his grave,
510    In the middle of nowhere. I wept. The wine,
Your wine, I opened it, poured him a mouthful,
Cut green leaves, olive, laid them there.
And then – there was a little altar,
Someone had killed a lamb, a black lamb,

Cut a lock of hair.
Death-offerings – but whose?
No one from Argos dares honour him.
Child, was it your brother?
Has Orestes come home in secret?
Visited the grave, in secret, wept?
Go there. Try the hair against your own,                    520
See if the colour matches.
Brother, sister: it might, it happens.

ELEKTRA.
You're talking about Orestes, uncle,
Brave Orestes. He'd have come openly:
He's not afraid. Of Aigisthos?
In any case, how could they match?
His hair's an athlete's, a gentleman's,
Hard and strong; mine's a woman's,
Soft with combing. Lots of people's hair matches        530
Who aren't related. It's nonsense, uncle.

OLD MAN.
The footprints, in the dust, beside the grave:
Go there, match them against yours.

ELEKTRA.
There's no dust there. It's rock.
And how could our footprints match –
A man's, a woman's? His feet would be bigger.

OLD MAN.
You're right. We'll not recognise him that way.
I know! He'll be wearing some garment
You made for him years ago,
I smuggled him to safety in.                                540

ELEKTRA.
When Orestes went into exile, I was a little girl.
Even if I had made him a 'garment',
He was a child then. It'd hardly fit him now –
Unless by some miracle, it grew while he did.
This is a stranger, uncle, a stranger.
He pitied my father, cut a lock of hair.
Or it's someone from Argos,

Slipping past the guards . . .

OLD MAN.
Your visitors, then: where are your visitors?
I want to ask them about Orestes.

ELEKTRA.
They're coming. They've heard you. They're here.

*Enter* ORESTES *and* PYLADES.

OLD MAN (*aside*).
550   They look princely enough. If looks were all,
If we could trust what people look like. Ah well.
(*Aloud.*) My lords, good morning.

ORESTES.
Good morning, old man.
(*Aside to* ELEKTRA.) Who's this old relic?
Whose side is he on?

ELEKTRA.
I told you. This is Father's old servant.

ORESTES.
The one who saved your brother?

ELEKTRA.
If Orestes is alive, it's thanks to him.

ORESTES.
What's he staring at? I'm not a coin:
Is he checking I'm real?

ELEKTRA.
He's pleased to see you,
560   Because you know Orestes.

ORESTES.
None better. Why is he walking round me?

ELEKTRA.
I've no idea.

OLD MAN.
Elektra, my dear, on your knees, child,
Pray, child . . .

ELEKTRA.
Why?

OLD MAN.
Ask God to let you hold, cherish forever –
A miracle.

ELEKTRA.
What are you talking about?

OLD MAN.
Look, child, open your eyes: your darling.

ELEKTRA.
What's wrong with you?

OLD MAN.
It's your brother. Your brother.

ELEKTRA.
Don't be silly. Is it?                                    570

OLD MAN.
Prince Orestes, Agamemnon's son.

ELEKTRA.
How can you tell?

OLD MAN.
A scar: look, there.
He fell, once. He was just a little boy.
You were trying to catch a fawn,
The pair of you. He fell.

ELEKTRA.
I see a scar, certainly.

OLD MAN.
So kiss him, hug him. After all these years.

ELEKTRA.
I believe you! The lock of hair, the footprints –
O Orestes, after all these years . . .
I never dared hope . . .

ORESTES.
Hold me . . .

ELEKTRA.
After all these years.

ORESTES.
580   I never dared hope.

ELEKTRA.
You're really Orestes?

ORESTES.
Count on me.
If I catch the prey I'm here to hunt –
No, what am I saying? Of course I'll catch it.
If criminals were allowed to win,
Why would anyone ever believe in God again?

*Music.*

CHORUS.
He's come;
He's here.
Bright dawn,
Sky-shine,
Day-shine, here.
He lived away,
Long exile,
Now he's here, he's here.
God's listening,
Elektra, God hears,
590   God gives us hope.
Lift up your hands,
Lift up your voice,
Pray now, pray:
God send him there,
God give him Argos,
Your brother,
Home at last.

*Music ends.*

ORESTES.
Well. Enough hugging, kissing, for now.
Tell me, old man – how lucky you were here –
That murderer, Father's murderer, and her,

My mother's bedmate, how do I punish them?          600
What do people think in Argos?
Has Orestes friends still there,
Or am I bankrupt in that as in other things?
Should I go now, in daylight?
Should I wait till it's dark?
Who'll help me? I need to know.

OLD MAN.
Unfortunately, no one supports you.
You're an exile. Good fortune or bad,
No one wants to know. You're alone.
It's entirely in your hands: your fate, the city,          610
Your father's throne restored – all are up to you.

ORESTES.
I don't know what to do.

OLD MAN.
Kill Aigisthos. Kill your mother.

ORESTES.
Thank you. But how?

OLD MAN.
You'll never get inside the city.

ORESTES.
Aigisthos has guards?

OLD MAN.
Exactly. He's scared of you. Daren't sleep.

ORESTES.
So what do I do? Advise me.

OLD MAN.
There is one way.

ORESTES.
I'm listening.          620

OLD MAN.
As I was coming here, I saw Aigisthos.

ORESTES.
Where was he?

OLD MAN.
He has a training farm, down the road.

ORESTES.
I don't see how this helps.

OLD MAN.
He was preparing a sacrifice.

ORESTES.
For children, was it? *Has* he children?

OLD MAN.
They were getting a bull ready.

ORESTES.
Who were? Soldiers? Or merely slaves?

OLD MAN.
Palace servants. No soldiers.

ORESTES.
630   Would they know who I was?

OLD MAN.
They're slaves: I doubt it.

ORESTES.
What would they do if I killed him?

OLD MAN.
They'd join you. They're slaves.

ORESTES.
Just a case of getting close enough . . .

OLD MAN.
Stand by the altar, and watch the sacrifice.

ORESTES.
This training farm: it's beside the road?

OLD MAN.
If he sees you, he'll invite you.

ORESTES.
He'll be sorry if he does.

OLD MAN.
Well, once it starts, it's up to you.

ORESTES.
And what about my mother? Where is she?    640

OLD MAN.
When the dancing starts, she'll come.

ORESTES.
Why didn't she come before? With her . . . mate.

OLD MAN.
The townspeople don't like it.

ORESTES.
Seeing them together? I should think they don't.

OLD MAN.
It's recent still:
They remember her husband, and what she did.

ORESTES.
I'm to kill them both? Kill both of them?

ELEKTRA.
Leave Mummy to me. I'll see to Mummy.

ORESTES.
I'll deal with the other one.

ELEKTRA.
And you, old man, can help us both.

OLD MAN.
I hear and obey. Have you a plan for her?    650

ELEKTRA.
Go to Her Majesty. Tell her
I've just had a child, a baby boy.

OLD MAN.
How recently?

ELEKTRA.
Ten days ago. Say I need her.

OLD MAN.
How will that help you kill her?

ELEKTRA.
She won't stay away.
As soon as she hears, she'll come.

OLD MAN.
She'll want to look *after* you?

ELEKTRA.
To look at her grandson.
'Poor little peasant! Aah . . .'

OLD MAN.
I still don't follow.

ELEKTRA.
660    When she comes, she dies.

OLD MAN.
In there?

ELEKTRA.
Hell's antechamber.

OLD MAN.
Let me see it, God let me see it, before I die.

ELEKTRA.
First, *he* needs to be shown the way –

OLD MAN.
To Aigisthos' sacrifice. I'll show him.

ELEKTRA.
Then hurry to Klytemnestra, tell her what I said.

OLD MAN.
You've just had a child, a baby boy. I've got it.

ELEKTRA.
Orestes, it's beginning. Now, it's now.

ORESTES.
If someone just shows me where he *is*.

OLD MAN.
670    I'll take you there. Don't worry.

    *Music.*

ORESTES.
Zeus father, Zeus conqueror –

ELEKTRA.
Look down on us. Pity us –

**OLD MAN.**
Help them, Lord. They need you, Lord.

**ELEKTRA.**
Hera, Queen of Heaven, who protects our state –

**ORESTES.**
Hear us now, and help –

**ELEKTRA.**
For Agamemnon, grant death for death.

*They kneel and beat the ground.*

Mother Earth, hear us –

**ORESTES.**
Ghost of our father, hear us –

**ELEKTRA.**
Hear us, your children, hear and help.

**ORESTES.**
Bring an army of ghosts –

**ELEKTRA.**
All who died at Troy –                                         680

**ORESTES.**
Crowding now, hunting them, hating them.

**ELEKTRA.**
Father, she did it. She did it. Hear me.

**OLD MAN.**
It's all right, he hears. It's time.

**ELEKTRA** (*to* ORESTES).
Remember. It's simple: Aigisthos dies.
And if he doesn't, if something happens
And it's you who . . . I'm dead, be sure of that,        690
A knife in the guts, I'm dead.
Women, listen for news.
Be beacons, blaze news.
I'll be waiting, listening, knife in my hand.
If we fail in this, they'll never take me,
The ones I hate won't hurt me more.

*Exeunt all but* CHORUS. *Music.*

CHORUS.
 Two brothers,
 Atreus and Thyestes,
 Fought for the throne,
 The throne of Argos.
 And high in the hills,
700 The hills of Argos,
 Pan the shepherd-god,
 Pan the piper,
 Found a golden lamb,
 Found it, brought it,
 Gave it to Atreus.
 There on palace steps
 A herald stood.
 'People of Argos, come!
 Proof, living proof,
 Golden proof:
710 Atreus owns the lamb, he rules.
 Dance for him, dance for Atreus,
 Dance.' They danced.

 Altars, gold cloth,
 Altars draped for sacrifice.
 Fire, gold-gleaming,
 Sacrifice in Argos.
 Flutes blossomed,
 Blossomed in Argos,
 Soft music, songs,
 Songs for golden lamb.
 Thyestes frowned,
720 Turned to treachery,
 Slept with Atreus' wife,
 Stole the golden lamb,
 His brother's treasure.
 'People of Argos, come,'
 His herald cried.
 'See in his house, His Majesty,
 Golden proof, horned proof,
 Thyestes has the lamb, he rules.'

 Zeus saw.

Zeus hid the sun,
Hid dawn,
Held back the stars,                                            730
Reversed their orbits.
Until that day,
Sun rose in the west,
Drove eastwards –
No more, no more.
Now northern lands
Clutch clouds to themselves,
Clutch rain,
Southern lands
Made desert, parched.

A pretty myth. But hardly fact.
– Unbelievable! The sun
Switch courses,
Start travelling west not east                                 740
To help some unhappy mortal?
– Mind you, myths teach respect,
Respect for the gods.
She should have thought of that,
Klytemnestra should have thought of that,
Before she killed.

   *Dance, broken off in confusion.*

Listen!
– Shouting.
– Didn't you hear it?
– Groaning, like an earthquake.
– Again.
– It's happening.
– It's here.
– Elektra,                                                     750
Come out!
– It's here.

   *Enter* ELEKTRA.

ELEKTRA.
Friends. Yes? It's happening?

CHORUS.
A death-struggle. Listen.

ELEKTRA.
I hear it.

CHORUS.
It's happening.

ELEKTRA.
Who's winning? Who's dead? Orestes?

CHORUS.
They're shouting, all of them.

ELEKTRA.
I'm done for. Inside, the knife —

CHORUS.
Wait till you know.

ELEKTRA.
He's failed. Why don't they tell us?

CHORUS.
760     They'll tell us. Aigisthos, dead? They'll tell us.

*Enter* PYLADES.

PYLADES.
We've won. Women of Argos, won!
Orestes has won. Rejoice!
Aigisthos the murderer is dead. Thank God.

ELEKTRA.
Why should I trust you? Tell me who you are.

PYLADES.
You saw me. I was with your brother.

ELEKTRA.
I'm sorry. Yes, of course:
You're the same man.
Now, what did you say?
He's dead? That butcher, dead?

PYLADES.
770     Dead, yes. I'll say it again,
As often as you like.

ELEKTRA.
　　Zeus, Justice, you came, you came!
　　Tell me, every detail, how Aigisthos died.

PYLADES.
　　We went that way, up the track.
　　We came to a wide road,
　　Wide enough for two wagons to pass each other.
　　We followed it – and found Aigisthos.
　　In a grove of trees, cutting myrtle-leaves,
　　Making himself a wreath for the sacrifice.
　　He saw us. 'Morning,' he called.
　　'Good to see you. Where are you from?'　　　　　780
　　Lord Orestes answered, 'Thessaly,
　　And we're on our way to Olympia: we're pilgrims.'
　　'Stay here tonight,' Aigisthos said.
　　'No excuses: you're welcome.
　　I'm making a sacrifice, holding a banquet.
　　Be my guests, get up early tomorrow –
　　One day on your journey
　　Won't make all that difference.
　　This way, this way' –
　　He was shaking our hands, pulling us –　　　　　790
　　'Slaves, bring the gentlemen water
　　To wash their hands,
　　Then show them their places,
　　Beside the altar, there.'
　　Orestes said, 'We've washed,
　　In the stream, just now.
　　We're ready, Majesty:
　　If strangers can sacrifice here,
　　We're ready.' So that was agreed.
　　The slaves put down their spears
　　(Aigisthos' slaves I mean,
　　They'd been guarding their master),
　　And started getting things ready:
　　A bowl for the blood,　　　　　800
　　Baskets of grain, fires to boil water.
　　Noise, clatter everywhere.

　　Your mother's bedmate took

A handful of barley-grains
And threw them on the fire. He prayed:
'Nymphs of these hills, these pastures,
Grant our prayers. When Her Majesty my wife
Sacrifices, when I sacrifice, grant our prayers:
Long life, prosperity, death to our enemies.'
He meant Orestes; you.
Orestes made prayers of his own,
In secret, without a word:
810    'My father's throne, restored.'

Aigisthos took the knife from the basket,
Cut a hank of hair from the bullcalf's mane,
Burned it in the altar fire.
The slaves lifted the calf, shoulder-high,
And he cut its throat.
'So you're from Thessaly?' he said to Orestes.
'They say you're good at two things in Thessaly:
Horse-breaking and carving sacrifices.
Take the knife, show what you can do.'
It was a short, straight knife, razor-edged.
820    Orestes took it, tossed back his cloak,
Asked me to help.
He took one leg of the carcass,
Laid it bare to the bone with a single sweep,
Then flayed the hide, faster than a runner
Could make two circuits of the track.
He removed the innards.
Aigisthos took the organs,
Inspected them for omens.
The liver, deformed;
Gall-bladder, main artery, defective –
Bad luck, danger from visitors.
830    He frowned. Orestes said, 'What's the matter?'
'I've enemies,' Aigisthos said. 'Relatives.
Agamemnon's son, Orestes, I curse his name,
Intends to have me dead.'
'You're joking, Majesty. A king in royal state,
An exile – how can *he* hurt *you*?
I'll finish the carcass. This knife's too small:

If we're to feast tonight, I need a longer blade
To separate the ribs.'

They gave him one. He split the ribs.
Aigisthos bent over them,
Holding them apart, and Orestes stabbed     840
Down, down, shattered his spine.
His whole body screamed: death-agony.
The slaves ran for their weapons.
Orestes and I were two; they were many.
Orestes said, 'Friends: we're your friends.
I'm Orestes.
This man killed my father; I punished him.
Faithful servants, Agamemnon's servants,
Will *you* kill *me*?' They lowered their spears.     850
An old man, he'd been a family slave for years,
Recognised Orestes.
Wild cheering, shouting,
Crowning with flowers.
He's coming, now.
The monster's dead –
No Gorgon, Aigisthos.
His debts are paid,
Blood pays for blood:
Orestes has his head.

   *Music.*

CHORUS.
  Dance, Elektra, dance,     860
  Leap like a fawn.
  Orestes has won –
  Crown him,
  Crown him.
  Dance. Sing. Dance.

ELEKTRA.
  Light of day,
  Sun-chariot,
  Mother Earth,
  Dark night that dulled my eyes,
  Freedom!

My eyes feast on it,
I shout it: freedom,
Aigisthos the murderer is dead.
870   Crowns, crowns in the house,
Fetch crowns for Orestes, crowns.

CHORUS.
Fetch them.
We'll wait for him,
Dance for him.
He killed
Our tyrant,
Won back his throne.
Dance for him. Dance.

*They dance.* ELEKTRA *fetches crowns from the
house. Enter* ORESTES *carrying* AIGISTHOS'
*head. Music ends.*

ELEKTRA.
880   Welcome. Accept this crown, Prince Orestes,
Son of the warlord who toppled Troy.
You ran the hard race, you triumphed,
You killed him, killed him, Aigisthos our enemy.
He murdered our father, and for that he died.
Pylades, accept this crown,
Noblest of friends, comrade, fine father's son.
You ran this race with him, won with him –
Live forever, twin princes, my princes, live.

ORESTES.
890   Gods first, Elektra. Their hand was here.
Praise to the gods, and then to us,
Their servants, servants of Fate.
I killed Aigisthos.
I said I would; I did.
I'll prove it: look.
Do what you like with this:
Throw it to dogs,
Spike it for birds. It's yours.
He ruled you once,
And now he's in your hands.

**ELEKTRA.**

All I want to do is . . . I can't. I'm embarrassed.          900

**ORESTES.**

Do it. Whatever you like: you're free.

**ELEKTRA.**

I want to shout at him. He's dead; I can't.

**ORESTES.**

Who'd blame you?

**ELEKTRA.**

Our Argives, our citizens.

**ORESTES.**

You're Orestes' sister. Their tyrant's dead.
We do as we like. We've finished it.

**ELEKTRA.**

All right.
You. Are you listening? All ears?
I'll say it all. Start where I want to start,
Say it all, end where I want to end.
Ten years, day after day, I've practised this.
Rehearsed it, said it to morning sun.
I'd have said it to your face, you terrorised us;          910
Now you're dead, I'll say it, it's yours.

You killed us. Orestes and me:
We did you no harm, you killed us.
You mated with our mother,
Kept well away from Troy,
Butchered Agamemnon, our father,
Grand Admiral of Greece.
What were you thinking of?
'Her Majesty, I'm her husband, she'll love me,
She'll be a true and loving wife.' It's like this:          920
Once an adulterer, always an adulterer –
If a woman betrays one husband,
She'll betray them all.
No peace in the house, no peace for you.
Had you really no idea of the life you led,
Of the pair you were: a murderer, an adulterer –

You deserved each other, smeared each other,
You were each what the other one deserved.
Aigisthos and Klytemnestra! D'you know
930      What your people called you? Husband and wife?
No: 'That woman and her . . . fancy-man'.
She ruled the roost. You were nothing.
What children did you have? *She* had children,
You had none. What were you?
A climber on the make,
A husband no-husband, a man no-man,
And you didn't even notice.
As for your well-known charm,
Your way with words, your silver tongue –
940      It was money talking, Agamemnon's money.
Fair-weather friends, all you ever made.
True character lasts, not money lasts.
A noble nature shelters us,
Protects us from storms, endures;
Ill-gotten gains fly out of the window,
They flower and die.

As for your women: I'm 'an innocent girl',
Shouldn't talk of such things. I blush to mention
    them.
God's gift, you thought yourself: His Majesty,
So handsome, so rich, so charming . . .
You'd nothing. You were good at dancing. Nothing.
Women dream of men, real men,
950      Having sons with men, not, not . . .
You didn't even notice:
Your whole life condemned you,
And you didn't notice.
You're a warning to the world:
Do what you like, live how you like,
Treat justice how you like,
But you're running a race,
And it's longer than you think.

CHORUS.
Pure wickedness, uncaring crime –
But Justice found him out in time.

ELEKTRA.
 I've done. Take it inside. Hide it:
 She mustn't see it, Mother mustn't see it,     960
 Until she sees the knife – then let her see.

 *The head is removed.*

ORESTES.
 Hurry. It's happening.

ELEKTRA.
 Someone's coming, from Argos. Soldiers.

ORESTES.
 No. It's her: my mother –

ELEKTRA.
 Stepping into the noose.
 What a glittering chariot!
 What gorgeous clothes!

ORESTES.
 What will we do? Not . . . kill her?

ELEKTRA.
 You're shaking. You see her, you're shaking.

ORESTES.
 Feoo.
 I can't kill her. My own mother.
 Her womb, her breast –

ELEKTRA.
 She murdered our father, yours and mine. She dies.    970

ORESTES.
 Apollo, is *this* what you ordered?

ELEKTRA.
 D'you challenge him?

ORESTES.
 But to kill my own mother –

ELEKTRA.
 To avenge your father –

ORESTES.
 And destroy myself –

ELEKTRA.
If you don't, if you disobey God's orders –

ORESTES.
If I kill her, her Furies will hunt me down.

ELEKTRA.
If you don't, Apollo will hunt you down.

ORESTES.
It wasn't Apollo.
It was a phantom, a fiend from Hell.

ELEKTRA.
980    On Apollo's throne of prophecy? Ridiculous.

ORESTES.
He can't have meant *this*. I misunderstood.

ELEKTRA.
Don't be such a coward.

ORESTES.
I'm to creep up on her, stab her –

ELEKTRA.
As she and Aigisthos killed our father.

ORESTES.
It's up to me. I'll do it.
God wants it. It's horrible.
God orders it. I must.

> *He and* PYLADES *go in. Music. Enter*
> KLYTEMNESTRA, *in a chariot, with*
> *Attendants.*

CHORUS.
Eeoh!
Lady, Majesty of Argos,
Tyndareos' daughter,
990    Sister of Kastor, of Polydeukes,
Zeus' sons who live in brightness,
Sun-dazzle, who save sailors' lives at sea,
Welcome, welcome. Majesty,
Like a god you are, joy, wealth, happiness.
You bless the ground you walk on;

You come here, and all is well. Welcome, welcome.

KLYTEMNESTRA (*to her Attendants*).
Help me down, then, out of the chariot.
Look, Elektra: my slaves,
The prettiest spoils of Troy.                                   1000
Its gold adorns our temples;
These beauties are mine,
Small compensation for your sister Iphigeneia,
My child who was stolen, but charming, charming.

ELEKTRA.
Mother, take my hand. I'll help you –
Another of your slaves, another possession.
Let me help Your Majesty.

KLYTEMNESTRA.
It's quite all right.
I brought my slaves on purpose.

ELEKTRA.
I'm not a slave, is that what you mean?
Dragged into exile, father murdered –
That happened to them, it happened to me.        1010

KLYTEMNESTRA.
Your father's to blame.
He betrayed the ones he loved;
He's to blame. I know what you're thinking:
'More lies, more slander – how can she say
Such things?' I know what you think of me.
But before people condemn people out of hand,
They ought to hear the facts, ought to listen,
Then despise with good reason, or not at all.

When I came to your father, Agamemnon,
I thought he was a husband, not a murderer.
But he took my child, Iphigeneia, he span
Some yarn about betrothing her to Achilles,       1020
Took her to Aulis where the fleet was,
Swung her high, slashed her throat,
Her innocent white throat.
Oh, I could have forgiven him –
If he'd done it to save our Argos,

If one child had to die to save others' lives.
But for her, for Helen? A bitch, a whore,
Out of all control, who slept with anyone –
For her he kills my daughter?
1030   Well, I bit my tongue. I could have killed him then,
I didn't – and then home from Troy he brings
Kassandra, the mad one, good at prophecy
And good in bed. Claims the palace is big enough:
Two wives, no problem.

So I found a lover of my own. What of it?
Women do that. My daughter murdered,
My husband an adulterer – what do they expect?
And who gets the blame? We do. Women do.
1040   Wives do. Who ever blames the husband?
Suppose Menelaos had been stolen to Troy,
Not Helen, Menelaos –
Would I have killed Orestes to get back
Helen's husband, my sister's husband?
If I'd laid one finger on Agamemnon's son,
He'd have killed me, my own husband
Would have killed me. Well, he took my daughter –
He had to die; I had to kill him.
And because none of his family,
None of you, would help, I turned to an outsider:
Aigisthos. He was handy.

Well? Say something. It's allowed;
You may speak. I know how you'll start:
1050   'My father did *not* deserve to die.'

CHORUS.
Every word you say is true, and every word is false.
You were his wife, you owed him loyalty,
You betrayed him – what else is there to say?

ELEKTRA.
Mother. 'It's allowed,' you said.
'You may speak,' you said.
Remember that: you gave permission.

KLYTEMNESTRA.
Well, child, of course I did.

ELEKTRA.
> To say what I like?

KLYTEMNESTRA.
> Whatever your heart desires.

ELEKTRA.
> In that case . . . First of all, Mother,  1060
> I wish you were . . . not what you are –
> Helen and Klytemnestra, sisters, beauties, whores.
> How Kastor your brother must blush for you!
> Aunt Helen was snatched by force, they say?
> She couldn't wait.
> You killed the finest man in Greece,
> Invented a reason afterwards:
> 'I killed him to avenge my child' –
> Other people may believe you; I don't.
> He'd hardly left the house, Agamemnon:
> Long before Iphigeneia's death
> Was even thought of, he'd hardly left the house  1070
> And there you were, primping and preening.
> Such pretty hair! A husband goes to war,
> And his wife runs to the mirror –
> What are we supposed to think?
> She's going to stay indoors?
> Or step outside, start hunting?
> And for you, it worked.
> I think you were the only wife in Greece to sulk
> When things went badly for the Trojans.
> You didn't want him back.
> What was wrong with you?  1080
> Agamemnon and Aigisthos –
> How could they possibly be compared,
> Aigisthos and the man chosen above all others
> To lead all Greece? You sister was a whore;
> You didn't need to join her. When people looked
> At her, and then at you, they should have cheered.
>
> Another thing. Agamemnon killed your daughter.
> *He* did it. What did *I* do? What did Orestes do?
> You killed your husband, ruler of Argos –
> Why didn't you give us our rights at once,

Our inheritance? You gave it to your bedmate,
1090 Payment for services rendered.
For what Aigisthos did to us,
He should be dead, be exiled:
Exiled for Orestes, dead for the living death
He gave me, far worse than anything
Iphigeneia suffered. Death pays for death,
You say. All right. You killed my father,
Orestes' father – and for that, you die.

KLYTEMNESTRA.
I'll tell you how it is.
1100 You're Daddy's girl, not Mummy's,
Always have been, always will be.
I forgive you.
It's not as if I take pride in what I did.
Child, I was furious: the heat of the moment,
1110 My own husband, I went a little far.

ELEKTRA.
It's too late now. He's dead, Father's dead.
But Orestes is alive, in exile.
You could bring him home.

KLYTEMNESTRA.
I daren't. Put yourself in my place.
His father's dead. He'll hate me.

ELEKTRA.
You could call Aigisthos off,
Stop him tormenting me.

KLYTEMNESTRA.
It isn't easy. When he makes up his mind . . .
He's just like you.

ELEKTRA.
Oh, I'm sorry. I'll change, I'll smile.

KLYTEMNESTRA.
Then so will he, perhaps.

ELEKTRA.
1120 Too late. He lives where I should live.

**KLYTEMNESTRA.**
You see: you always start again.

**ELEKTRA.**
Oh, I'll be quiet. He scares me: quiet!

**KLYTEMNESTRA.**
Let's leave it. You asked me to come. Why?

**ELEKTRA.**
The baby: they told you, I've had a baby.

**KLYTEMNESTRA.**
Some time ago, several days ago.
You might at least have washed,
Combed your hair. There's no excuse for –

**ELEKTRA.**
Do something for me: sacrifice.
When a baby's born, we sacrifice,
Ask for good omens. I don't know the words,
I've never done this before. Please help.

**KLYTEMNESTRA.**
Can't you ask the midwife?

**ELEKTRA.**
I delivered him. I was on my own.                    1130

**KLYTEMNESTRA.**
You don't have neighbours here?

**ELEKTRA.**
No one comes. We're poor.

**KLYTEMNESTRA.**
Oh all right.
I'll go inside, pay the gods their due –
Because you ask so prettily.
Then I'll go up the road.
Aigisthos is sacrificing:
There's to be a banquet,
Somewhere on the estate.
Slaves, feed the horses, water them.
I won't be long. Wait for me here,
I'll do what has to be done.

(*To* ELEKTRA.) First you, then Aigisthos.
I oblige everyone.

ELEKTRA.
1140    This way. Mind your dress: the walls are sooty.
Go in. The gods are waiting. Make your sacrifice.

    *Exit* KLYTEMNESTRA.

It's waiting too, the knife. It killed that bull,
It'll drink your blood. You'll lie by his side,
Mated in life, in death. You'll lie with him in Hell.
I, too, grant favours. Blood for blood.

    *Exit. Music.*

CHORUS.
Blood for blood.
Winds change, tides change.
In this stricken house, all changes.
Long ago he died,
Agamemnon, my Agamemnon,
1150    Crying out in the bath-house,
'Wife, bitch-wife,
Who cuts me down,
Ten years I fought
In Troy, for this, for this!'

Blood for blood.
Tides change.
She lifted her hand,
Red hand, sharp axe,
She cut him down,
1160    Her lord, home in his fortress,
Agamemnon.
What crime, what guilt, was his?
A lioness she was, stalking:
In forest glades, orchards,
She stalked, she pounced.

KLYTEMNESTRA (*inside*).
Children, in God's name, your mother, no!

CHORUS.
Shouting, inside.

KLYTEMNESTRA (*inside*).
Eeoh moee moee.

CHORUS.
They're hurting her,
Poor lady.
– Her children,
Hurting her.
– Justice, she earned it.
Blood for blood.
– Her husband's blood.
– They're coming.
Wading in blood,
Blood-hands, blood-steps,
Blood shrieks what they did,
Their tears, their triumph.
– What house ever suffered
As this house suffers?

*Enter* ORESTES *and* ELEKTRA, *with the body.*

ORESTES.
Zeus! Mother Earth!
Look. All human life you see,
See this. I killed them.
They hurt me, I killed them.

ELEKTRA.
Weep, weep tears.
I blazed, she died.
Our mother died. I did it.

CHORUS.
Weep for her,
Mother of pain,
Mother of tears –
– She earned it.
She killed, she died.

ORESTES.
Apollo, look!
'Kill,' you said. I didn't know,
Didn't understand.
I killed my mother, I'm dead,

1170

1180

1190

I'm banished from Greece,
From all who fear the gods.
Who'll help me?

ELEKTRA.
Eeoh eeoh moee.
Who'll dance for me now,
1200    Who'll welcome me, marry me?

CHORUS.
Wind changes,
Tides change.
Before, you defied the gods;
Now you obey, you understand.
Elektra, you made him do it:
Your brother, you made him do it.

ORESTES.
Did you see, inside? I knocked her down,
She opened her dress, gave her breast;
I struck, her dress tore open, I saw
Where I was born. Eeoh moee. I took her hair —

CHORUS.
We heard.
1210    Ee ee eeoh.
Shrieking, agony,
Your mother.

ELEKTRA.
She was screaming,
Reaching, touching.
'Don't hurt me.
Don't hurt Mummy. Please.'
She clung. She hugged me,
Arms round my neck.
I dropped the knife. She hung from me.

CHORUS.
How could you bear it, watch
1220    Blood bubbling, your mother's blood?

ORESTES.
I lifted my cloak, hid my eyes,

Sacrifice, knife, cut throat, blood, mother . . .

ELEKTRA.
'Now!' I said. 'Now!'
I touched the knife, I pushed it . . .

CHORUS.
How could you bear it?

ORESTES.
Cover her. Make her neat,
Close her wounds.
She gave us life. We killed her . . .

ELEKTRA (*to the body*).
Sleep now, sleep.                                    1230
We loved you. We killed you. Sleep.

CHORUS.
So it ends. Pain ends.

No. There.
– Shining, there.
– Gods shining in the sky.
– Gods, shining, to mortal eyes
Made manifest.

    *Enter* KASTOR *and* POLYDEUKES. *Music
    ends.*

KASTOR.
Orestes, Prince of Argos, hear us: Zeus' sons,
Your mother's brothers, Kastor, Polydeukes,          1240
Mortals once, now gods, our job to calm the sea.
We came to Argos. We watched you kill
Our sister, your mother. She deserved to die.
But the guilt is yours. Apollo spoke –
Our Lord, we don't blame Apollo –
But what he said was wrong.
It's happened, it can't be changed. Now hear
What Zeus and the Fates ordain for you.

Elektra's to marry Pylades,
And you're to run from Argos.                         1250
A mother-murderer, how could you stay?
Dog-goddesses, Furies, will hunt you down,

Steal your wits, send you wandering, wandering,
Till you come to Athens, Athene's temple.
Find her statue there, touch it, hug it:
She'll hold them off, their dragon-tongues,
She'll shelter you.
There's a court in Athens, the Areiopagos,
Where the first murder-trial on earth was held –
1260   After Ares the wargod killed Halirrothios,
Poseidon's son, who raped his daughter.
Ever since, no other place
Has been so respected, by mortals, gods.
There you'll stand jury trial, for murder.
The votes will be equal. You'll be acquitted.
Apollo, who ordered your mother's death,
Will take all the blame of it. And so it will be
Forever: equal votes in a verdict
Will bring acquittal, always.

Shrieks of rage, pain at your acquittal:
1270   The Furies will settle in a cleft, deep in the rock,
Under that hill – a place of dread,
Of respect, for always. As for you,
You'll settle in Arkadia, by the river:
You'll found a city – Oresteion, your own.

That's what you'll do.
The townspeople here
Will take Aigisthos' corpse and bury it.
Helen and Menelaos are sailing here;
They're on their way,
1280   They'll bury your mother.
In fact, Helen never went to Troy:
It was all a dream.
God stole her away to Egypt,
Sent a phantom in her place to Troy,
To tear the world apart.
Send Pylades with Elektra home to Phokis,
To marriage in Phokis. Send the farmer with him,
The one they called your brother-in-law:
Let him go with them, be honoured,
Be showered with riches.

Orestes, you, start running:
Run from the Furies, run
Till you come to Athens, 1290
Till the stain begins to fade, till happiness.

*Music.*

ELEKTRA.
Lord. Son of Zeus.
Hear me.

KASTOR.
Speak; it's allowed.

ELEKTRA.
I kneel to you.

KASTOR.
You did as Apollo ordered.

ELEKTRA.
You were Klytemnestra's brothers.
You knew she was to die —
Why didn't you prevent it? 1300

KASTOR.
Fate demanded it.
Apollo, rashly, ordered it.

ELEKTRA.
I had no orders.
God didn't order me to kill.

KASTOR.
You shared it: one crime,
One guilt, one madness.

ORESTES.
Elektra, I longed for you.
All these years, I needed you.
Now I find you, I lose you. 1310

KASTOR.
She has a home, a husband,
No cause to weep —
Unless, perhaps, for Argos.

ELEKTRA.
To leave one's home, one's birthplace!

ORESTES.
You drive me from Argos
To stand trial for my mother
Among strangers?

KASTOR.
1320    It's Athene's city. She'll protect you.

ELEKTRA.
Orestes, hold me.
We have to part.
Fate drives us apart,
Her blood. She's won.

ORESTES.
Hold me. Kiss me.
I'm dead: weep tears for me.

KASTOR.
Feoo feoo. This is very sad.
Gods weep for you. I weep.
1330    For mortals, look! gods weep.

ORESTES.
I'll never see you again.

ELEKTRA.
Never again.

ORESTES.
Never speak to you.

ELEKTRA.
Argos, farewell,
Dear friends, farewell.

ORESTES.
You're going already?

ELEKTRA.
I'm weeping. I'm going.

ORESTES.
1340    Pylades, take her, marry her.
Goodbye.

*Exeunt* PYLADES *and* ELEKTRA.

KASTOR.
    They've a marriage to plan.
    And you've those dogs
    To think about: those Furies,
    Skins of darkness, snake-bracelets –
    They'll sniff you out, they'll hunt you down.
    You're theirs! Unless you run now, you're theirs!

    *Exit* ORESTES.

    We're off now. Ships to protect –
    An Athenian expeditionary force, to Sicily.
    We sail through the sky, we part the clouds,
    For honest folk, not criminals.               1350
    If you respect the law, respect the gods.
    If you never go to sea with criminals,
    We'll help you. Remember that. God speaks.

    *Exeunt* KASTOR *and* POLYDEUKES.

CHORUS.
    Sons of Zeus, farewell.
    And may all of us fare well
    In the race of life, not stumble,
    Run free at last, to happiness.

    *Exeunt.*

# ORESTES

*translated by Kenneth McLeish*

# Characters

ELEKTRA
HELEN
ORESTES
MENELAOS
TYNDAREOS
PYLADES
OLD MAN
HERMIONE
TROJAN (dialect part)
APOLLO
SOLDIERS, ATTENDANTS (non-speaking)
CHORUS OF WOMEN OF ARGOS

*Argos, outside* AGAMEMNON's *former palace.*
ORESTES, *sick, sleeps on a mattress.* ELEKTRA *is
beside him.*

ELEKTRA.
　Disaster, pain, plague, misery,
　Whatever the gods choose to heap on us –
　The human condition. We shoulder it.
　Tantalos, for example. Zeus' son, they say.
　Tantalos the blessed – I'm not making fun of him –
　Cowering in midair, stone looming overhead,
　Threatening – and why? What for?
　He was a guest, they say,
　A mortal guest at some party of the gods,
　And forgot himself, went far too far.
　It's dreadful; it happens.                                    10

　Another one:
　Atreus, Tantalos' grandson, Pelops' son –
　What else did the spinning Fates choose for him
　But war? With his own brother too.
　Atreus and Thyestes! I needn't go on,
　Don't want to go on. Asks his brother to dinner:
　Dead baby stew, his brother's babies.

　Passing over what happened next,
　We come to Atreus' sons, Agamemnon –
　Glorious Agamemnon, if glorious is the word –
　And Menelaos. Their mother's name? Airope:
　Airope the Cretan. Menelaos married Helen
　(The one the gods detest), and Lord Agamemnon
　Married Klytemnestra –                                        20
　A catch, all Greece thought that.
　Three girls they had – Chrysothemis, Iphigeneia,
　Me (Elektra, yes) – and one boy, Orestes.
　Agamemnon's children, and hers,
　That bitch, that foulness,
　Who wrapped her own husband in a woven net
　And killed him? Why? I'm an innocent virgin,
　Know nothing of marriage, it's not for me to say,
　You work it out.

So we come to Apollo, Phoebus Apollo.
Not to blame the god,
But he did persuade Orestes
To kill his own mother,
30      Not the most popular crime in all the world.
Orestes did what he was told,
What God told him. I helped,
As much as a woman could –
And so did Pylades:
He was one of us, he helped.
That's the story so far.
That's why Orestes is there,
Poor Orestes, sick on that bed. Raging fever,
Gnawing, hounded into madness
By his mother's blood – I won't speak their names,
The goddesses, who're hunting him, haunting
         him . . .
Six days now,
40      Six days since we butchered our mother,
Burned her in cleansing fire – and in all that time
He hasn't washed, hasn't eaten.
He cowers in those blankets.
When he's not having fits, when he's sane,
He sobs. Then he's up.
Running, running, an unbridled colt.

They've passed a decree about us,
The citizens of Argos:
No one's to shelter us, feed us, speak to us,
The matricides. And today
They're to take a second vote,
A community decision: will they stone us to death
50      Or leave us to cut each other's throats?

Oh, we've hope. We may escape.
Menelaos has landed, back at last from Troy.
His warship's moored by the headland.
He got lost, after the war, the Trojan War,
Got lost, wandered everywhere.
She's here too, Helen Hell-to-Men.
He sent her ahead, under cover of darkness,

Didn't want her seen in daylight,
By any of those whose sons lie dead in Troy,
Didn't want her stoned. She's inside,                    60
Weeping for Klytemnestra (her sister, after all)
And all the other royal disasters. She's all right:
She's got her daughter to comfort her, Hermione,
The child Menelaos left at home
When he sailed for Troy –
He brought her here to Sparta, entrusted her
To Klytemnestra, our mother, to bring her up.
Helen has Hermione, she can laugh, forget.

I'm watching the road, this way, that way,
For Menelaos. If he doesn't come,
If he doesn't help us, we're finished.
'There's naught so hapless as a Fate-struck house.'    70

    *Enter* HELEN.

HELEN.
Elektra, virgin – still virgin –
Daughter of Agamemnon and Klytemnestra,
Poor soul, how are you,
And your brother Orestes,
Unfortunate Orestes who killed his own mother?
See: I can talk to you, I'm not contaminated.
I blame Apollo anyway. What a dreadful thing
To happen to Klytemnestra! My own sister!
I sailed for Troy, never saw her again.
I had to sail. God made me;
It was Fate; I'd no other choice.
And now she's gone, and all I have is tears.           80

ELEKTRA.
Helen, see for yourself – no need to tell you –
The two of us: Agamemnon's son, destroyed,
A corpse, a breathing corpse,
And me, chief mourner. You've done all right,
Menelaos has done all right –
And Orestes and I, we've come to this.

HELEN.
He's been lying there – how long?

ELEKTRA.
Since he . . . bloodied his mother.

HELEN.
90   Poor soul. And her as well, poor soul.

ELEKTRA.
It happened. It's how it is.

HELEN.
I wonder, darling, would you do me a favour?

ELEKTRA.
I'm rather busy. Sitting here with him.

HELEN.
Would you go to her grave instead of me – ?

ELEKTRA.
Whose grave? *Her* grave? Whatever for?

HELEN.
To make offerings. These dishes . . . this lock of
    hair . . .

ELEKTRA.
She was your sister. It's for you to go.

HELEN.
I'm embarrassed.
I daren't show my face in Argos –

ELEKTRA.
You should have thought of that before.

HELEN.
100   That's true. Unkind, but true.

ELEKTRA.
You say you're embarrassed – why?

HELEN.
They'll see me: the parents whose sons died *there*.

ELEKTRA.
Your name's on every lip.

HELEN.
So if you'd . . . I mean, if you wouldn't mind . . .

ELEKTRA.
You think *I* could bear it? My mother's grave?

HELEN.
One can't ask a slave –

ELEKTRA.
What about Hermione? Your daughter.

HELEN.
She's a young girl. She can't go out alone.

ELEKTRA.
She owes honour
To the woman who brought her up.

HELEN.
You're right, darling. I'll do it, I'll send her.          110
Hermione, sweetheart, come out here.

   *Enter* HERMIONE.

Take these dishes, this lock of hair –
Mummy's hair. Go to Klytemnestra's grave.
Sprinkle the offerings: milk, wine, honey.
Then stand bravely on the grave and say,
'Helen, your sister, sends these offerings.
She'd have come in person, but the problem was:
The people.' Ask her to bless us all –
Me, you, Daddy, this unhappy pair          120
Destroyed by the gods. Promise her
I'll give her all the grave-gifts we owe the dead –
I will, I will. Hurry, sweetheart,
And when you've finished, come and tell me.

   *Exit* HERMIONE. HELEN *goes inside.*

ELEKTRA.
Human nature! What a curse it is –
Except for the lucky ones!
Did you see that hair she offered –
Clipped at the side, so as not to spoil her looks?
She hasn't changed. God damn you, damn you          130
For leaving Orestes, me, Greece, like this!

Oh no. Here they are again: my friends.

They're going to sing again. They'll wake him up;
He'll rave again; I'll watch him and weep again.

*Enter* CHORUS.

Friends, shh! Quietly.
Tiptoe. It's very kind of you,
But if you wake him up, I'm dead.

*Music.*

CHORUS.
140    Hush now, hush. Tread gently.
Walk with silent step.
Be quiet.

ELEKTRA.
Not that way, please. Not beside the bed.

CHORUS.
She's right. This way.

ELEKTRA.
Ah, ah, like breath of flute,
Softly, oh softly, sing your song.

CHORUS.
Softly, oh softly, sing our song.

ELEKTRA.
That's right.
Come this way, come.
That's right.
What d'you want?
150    What's brought you?
He hasn't slept like this in days.

CHORUS.
How is he? Tell us. Please:
We're friends. How is he?

ELEKTRA.
Breathing – just. He pants, he groans.

CHORUS.
Poor soul, poor soul.

ELEKTRA.
Sleep's sweetness soothes his eyes.
If you wake him, if he wakes, I'm dead.

CHORUS.
God crushes him. Poor man!                    160

ELEKTRA.
He's trapped.
Bitter, bitter, that day
When Apollo enthroned, commanded:
'She killed, the mother, kill her.'

CHORUS.
Look: the blankets. He moved.

ELEKTRA.
It's your fault: your noise.
You disturbed him.

CHORUS.
He's still asleep.

ELEKTRA.
Please go. Take your noise             170
And leave us. Go away.

CHORUS.
He's sleeping.

ELEKTRA.
Thank God.
Night, Lady Night,
You bless mortal eyes with sleep,
Up, up from the halls of dark,
Fly, fly to Agamemnon's house.
Disaster, suffering,                    180
We're lost, we're dead, oh – shh!
Be quiet, be quiet, back from the bed,
Please let the poor man sleep.

CHORUS.
What end is left for him?

ELEKTRA.
What else? He'll die.

He doesn't eat.

CHORUS.
190   There's no hope left.

ELEKTRA.
No hope.
Apollo, Lord,
You sacrificed us, made us victims,
Blood-sacrifice: father, mother, us.

CHORUS.
In Justice' name.

ELEKTRA.
How, Justice?
She killed, she died –
But what of us, her husband, her children?
What did we do? She killed us:
200   Her husband, her children, dead.
Her son lies like the dead;
Her daughter's life is nothing –
Weeping, weeping in the dark,
Unmarried, childless,
What's left for me?

CHORUS.
Elektra, check.
You're beside him, there.
He's dreadfully quiet.
210   Has he slipped away?

   ORESTES *stirs.*

ORESTES.
Beloved sleep, enchanter, healer,
How you smiled and came when I needed you.
Oblivion, lady, in trouble we pray to you,
And our prayers are answered.
Where am I? Where was I?
What's happened? I can't remember.

ELEKTRA.
You slept, darling. I was so happy.
Let me lift you, make you comfortable.

ORESTES.
    Please. Please. My lips . . . my eyes . . .
    Wipe away the froth . . .                          220

ELEKTRA.
    There. A slave's task, a pleasure:
    Sister helps brother, I'm glad to do it.

ORESTES.
    Hold me up. My hair's in my eyes,
    I can't see.

ELEKTRA.
    Poor hair, poor head,
    So tangled, so dirty.

ORESTES.
    Lay me down again.
    The fits leave me weak, no strength –

ELEKTRA.
    There. Bed-rest – it's a nuisance,
    But it's essential.                                230

ORESTES.
    Sit me up again. Turn me round.
    I'm sick, I don't know what I want.

ELEKTRA.
    Shall I help you stand? Take a step or two?
    It'd make a nice change.

ORESTES.
    I'll try.
    Even if I don't feel better,
    I'll pretend . . .

ELEKTRA.
    Now, listen, darling, it's important,
    While your head's clear, while the Furies let you . . .

ORESTES.
    You've news. If it's good, tell me;
    If it isn't, keep it. I've pain enough.            240

ELEKTRA.
    Menelaos is here, Uncle Menelaos.

His warship's moored at the headland.

ORESTES.
Menelaos: our light, our saviour.
He'll help us, as Father once helped him.

ELEKTRA.
He's come back, no doubt about it.
He's home from Troy, with Helen.

ORESTES.
He should have come alone, left her.
If *she's* here too, it's trouble.

ELEKTRA.
What a pair of daughters our grandfather had –
250    Klytemnestra, Helen, shame of his house!

ORESTES.
You be different. You *can*.
Say you'll be different. Promise.

ELEKTRA.
Orestes. . . ! His eyes are rolling.
Another fit. He seemed so well.

ORESTES.
Mother, on my knees, don't hit me, snakes,
Blood-eyes, they're here, they're here.

ELEKTRA.
Sh, sh. Lie down.
They're not here. There's no one here.

ORESTES.
260    Apollo, look, dogs, Hell's hunters,
Gorgons, they're after me.

ELEKTRA.
I've got you. I'll hold you.
Be still. Be calm.

ORESTES.
Let go. You're one of them,
You're dragging me down to Hell.

ELEKTRA.
Who'll help us? God crushes us.

Who'll help us now?

ORESTES.

    Give me my bow. Horn-sprung, Apollo's gift.
    'Take it,' he said, 'Shoot them, drive them away,
    If they swarm on you, if they try to get you.'    270
    D'you hear? Stay back! Stand clear!
    Feathered arrows, bow, springing –
    There's a goddess asking for trouble.
    Haar! Haar!
    Whirr of wings. Fly, fly. Apollo, blame Apollo,
    He told me to do it, don't blame me.

    Ea.
    What's happening? I can't breathe.
    Where am I? I was lying in bed.
    The storm's settling; there's calm ahead.
    Elektra, you've covered your face, you're crying:    280
    My fault. You should be a wife, a mother,
    Not nursing a brother, a madman.
    You said we should kill her, but you didn't do it,
    I did. This foulness: it was Apollo's fault. 'Kill,
        kill' –
    He gave me words, gave me promises, and failed me.
    What would Father have said, if I'd asked him,
    Looked him in the eyes and asked him,
    'Am I to kill her, kill my own mother, yes or no'. . . ?
    He'd have gone on his knees, begged me, begged,    290
    'Your mother, don't do it, don't cut her throat,
    It won't bring me back my life, it'll bring you pain.'
    Pain. This pain. Pain piled on pain . . .

    Don't cry, Elektra.
    Uncover your head.
    It's hard, it's hard.
    When I'm . . . not myself . . .
    Talk to me, comfort me,
    Talk me well again.
    I'll do the same for you.
    Kind words, loving words,
    A sister, a brother . . .    300
    Dearest, go in. Wash, eat, snatch sleep.

You're all I have, you're my only hope.
If you fall ill, if you desert me,
What's left for me?

ELEKTRA.
I'm here. Life, death, I'm here.
It comes to this:
What else do I have?
If you die, what's left for me —
A woman, alone,
Brotherless, unfathered, friendless —
310   What's left for me?
I'll go in, if it's what you want.
Lie down. And if it comes again,
The panic, stay there.
Don't get up. It may be real . . .
Imagination . . . but whichever it is,
Don't fight it, don't exhaust yourself.

   *Exit. Music.*

CHORUS.
Aee aee.
Powers of dark,
You run on the wind,
Powerful ones,
320   Chuckling in tears;
Black Ones, Friendly Ones,
You swoop the sky,
Cry Justice, cry blood for blood.
We beg you, beg,
Set free this boy,
Agamemnon's son,
Unlock his mind,
Take away the madness.
He asked the oracle,
330   Apollo's oracle,
Navel of the world —
How could he know?

Eeoh Zeus!
Agony hunts him,

Tracks him,
Spurs him with tears,
Roars on him, floods him,
His mother's blood
Engulfing, swarming, haunting.
Weep for him, weep.
What's happiness?                                    340
It's dead, it's dead,
A tall ship, sailing,
Fate-drowned, swamped,
Swamped by the gods.
What royal house
Stood higher once than this,
And fell so far?

   *Music ends.*

Look: Menelaos. His Majesty.
How proud he is, how fine!
His Majesty's royal line!                             350

   *Enter* MENELAOS, *attended.*

Joy, joy! You launched a thousand ships,
Your army swarmed on Troy,
You prayed, God answered.
You've all you asked. Joy, joy!

MENELAOS.
Home. We fought; we're home.
We smile to see this palace: smile, and weep.
What house has suffered more?
Our brother Agamemnon – we were beaching            360
At Malia when they brought us news,
Told us his fate.
Glaukos spoke, voice of the sea-god,
Prophet, priest, infallible:
'Dead, lord, your brother's dead,
Bathed by his wife – the last bath he'll ever take.'
Our eyes filled with tears, the sailors wept.
I made my way to the headland,
Sent my wife ahead,
Made plans to shake my nephew's hand,               370

Orestes, son of Agamemnon, and his mother,
Klytemnestra, my sister-in-law,
In good health both.
Then came gossip in the harbour:
Her Majesty was dead, foully done to death.
You, women, where is he, Agamemnon's son?
He dared it, did it – where is he?
When I left for Troy, he was a baby in arms:
I'd hardly know him now.

ORESTES.

380 I'm here, Menelaos. Orestes: here.
I kneel at your feet, a suppliant.
I'll tell you everything:
Only you can help. You're in the nick of time.

MENELAOS.

Good God, who's this? A walking corpse?

ORESTES.

Exactly. I live, I see the sun, I'm dead.

MENELAOS.

But the state you're in! Your dirt, your hair.

ORESTES.

Dirt in the soul, lord, dirt in the heart.

MENELAOS.

Wild eyes, cold eyes – that stare!

ORESTES.

390 I'm dead, lord. I'm nothing but my name.

MENELAOS.

You've changed. I'm amazed –

ORESTES.

I killed my mother.

MENELAOS.

I had heard. Don't speak of it.

ORESTES.

My lord, the pain is mine.

MENELAOS.

Explain. What's wrong with you?

ORESTES.
Remorse. Conscience. Remembered guilt.

MENELAOS.
Do try to be specific.

ORESTES.
My conscience is gnawing me alive.

MENELAOS.
It does that. But it doesn't last.

ORESTES.
Madness, phantoms, my mother's blood.          400

MENELAOS.
Phantoms. Since when – I mean, what day?

ORESTES.
The day we built my mother's tomb.

MENELAOS.
Were you at home, or by the funeral pyre?

ORESTES.
At night. After the fire.
I was waiting till it cooled,
To gather the bones.

MENELAOS.
Were you alone?

ORESTES.
Pylades was there. My . . . strong right arm.

MENELAOS.
These phantoms. What are they like, exactly?

ORESTES.
Women . . . night-shapes . . . dark.

MENELAOS.
Don't name them. I know who you mean.

ORESTES.
The holy ones.          410

MENELAOS.
They swarm on you, you say, because you killed –

ORESTES.
My mother. They swarm, they hunt.

MENELAOS.
Foul crimes deserve foul punishment.

ORESTES.
There's only one way out.

MENELAOS.
What, kill yourself? What good would that do?

ORESTES.
I obeyed Apollo. He told me: kill her.

MENELAOS.
Rather a drastic view of justice.

ORESTES.
He's a god, if gods exist. They order; we obey.

MENELAOS.
And now you're suffering – where is he now?

ORESTES.
420       He'll come. They take their time.

MENELAOS.
How long since your mother . . . left us?

ORESTES.
Six days. The pyre's still warm.

MENELAOS.
*They* wasted no time, the bloodhounds.

ORESTES.
All I know is, I'm a loyal son.

MENELAOS.
You avenged your father. That's no help at all?

ORESTES.
Not yet – and that's as good as none.

MENELAOS.
And the people of Argos – how do they view this?

ORESTES.
With loathing. They turn away. No words.

MENELAOS.
Purgation-rituals – you've done all those?

ORESTES.
I'm barred: doors slammed in my face.                    430

MENELAOS.
They want you banished. Who, in particular?

ORESTES.
Oiax. He blames my father for . . .
What happened at Troy.

MENELAOS.
Palamedes' brother: it's reasonable.

ORESTES.
It wasn't my fault. And there are others.

MENELAOS.
Supporters of Aigisthos?

ORESTES.
They rule the town.

MENELAOS.
*They* rule? You're Agamemnon's son!

ORESTES.
The people want my blood.

MENELAOS.
What d'you mean?

ORESTES.
They've called a public vote, today.                     440

MENELAOS.
To exile you? To let you live, or die?

ORESTES.
To have me stoned to death.

MENELAOS.
Then why are you still here?

ORESTES.
The gates are guarded. Swords, spears, everywhere.

MENELAOS.
Aigisthos' followers, or others too?

ORESTES.
All Argos wants my death.
A whole city, united. That's all.

MENELAOS.
Things could hardly be worse.

ORESTES.
That's why I turn to you, lord. Help me.
450    You're home in the flush of success,
Unchallenged, prosperous – share it,
Help your own relatives, don't hug it all.
My father helped you, now pay that debt.
When troubles come,
It's then we know our friends.

CHORUS.
The old man's coming:
Tyndareos, dressed in black, hair shorn,
In mourning for his daughter.

ORESTES.
Menelaos, I'm dead. How can I face
460    Tyndareos, Mother's father, after what I did?
Grandfather! When I was a baby,
How he loved me. Carried me everywhere,
Called me 'Agamemnon's little prince',
Kissed me – and so did Leda, grandmother.
I was like the heavenly twins to them –
And see how I repaid them.
Where can I hide? How cover myself,
How avoid the old man's eyes?

    *Enter* TYNDAREOS, *attended*.

TYNDAREOS.
470    Where's Menelaos?
My daughter's husband, where?
I was at the grave, Klytemnestra's grave,
Making offerings. They said he'd come,
He was at the headland. Menelaos, Helen, home

After all these years! Take me to him.
I want to see him, hug him, shake his hand.

MENELAOS.
Father-in-law.

TYNDAREOS.
Menelaos! Son-in-law!
Ea.
Why didn't they tell me? *He's* here,
The snake-in-the-grass, the mother-biter, here,
Fire-eyes, poison-eyes, I spit on him.
Menelaos, you *speak* to him?                                    480

MENELAOS.
My own dear brother's son –

TYNDAREOS.
Impossible. A foundling.

MENELAOS.
His father's son. In trouble, but still my nephew.

TYNDAREOS.
You've been too long in Troy. You're soft.

MENELAOS.
To honour a kinsman? That's Greek, that's Greek.

TYNDAREOS.
And when the law says otherwise?

MENELAOS.
I hold to a greater law.

TYNDAREOS.
I want no part of it.

MENELAOS.
Then you're a fool, old man.                                    490

TYNDAREOS.
Why are we arguing? *He's* the point,
Right and wrong are the point.
Right and wrong, the law –
What did *he* ever care for those?
When did *he* ever appeal to Justice?
As soon as Agamemnon breathed his last –

Hit on the head by my daughter, I don't deny it –
*He* should have stuck to the law,
500     Ordained by the gods,
And banished his mother.
Just penalty; public praise
For keeping his head in a bad situation,
For piety. Instead,
He turns out just as bad as she was.
He judged her beyond the law for what she did –
And what does that make him, for what *he* did?
Imagine this, Menelaos:
One day *his* wife kills him, and the wife's son
510     Wipes out the murder with another –
How far down the line must we go to end it?
They did things so much better in the old days:
If you'd blood on your hands
You were a non-person, not seen,
Not spoken to. You were removed, not killed –
No endless repeating chain of death for death,
Pollution for pollution. Don't get me wrong:
Adulterers, murderers, I hate them all,
And Klytemnestra first of all – my own daughter,
Who killed her husband. Yes, and her sister,
Helen, she's a bad bargain, an adulterer,
520     I'm amazed you went to Troy for her,
I've nothing to say to her.
But I'm talking about the law.
I'll uphold it till I die.
We're not animals. Let's have an end to butchery:
It ruins cities, countries, let's have an end to it.
(*To* ORESTES.) Animals. Exactly.
When she bared her breast, your own mother,
When she begged for mercy – how could you do it?
I didn't see it, I picture it.
Tears fill these poor old eyes.
530     One thing, at least, proves what I say:
The gods hate you,
You're paying their price for what you did,
You're mad, wits blasted, terrified.
There's nothing more to say, Menelaos.

Look at him. If you help him,
You defy the gods. Leave him.
The people will stone him to death; let them.
Klytemnestra, my daughter, deserved to die –
But not to be killed by him. Daughters!
I had my share of human happiness –                           540
And then I had daughters, and see me now!

CHORUS.
How blest they are, whose children turn out well.
If not, they make your life a living hell.

ORESTES.
My lord . . . grandfather . . . I'm embarrassed.
You'll be furious, hurt, whatever I say.
Respect for you, respect for one's elders . . .
I must put it aside. I have to speak.
To kill your own mother, and break the law;
To avenge your own father, and keep the law –                 550
What sort of choice is that?
My father sowed the seed,
Your daughter accepted it,
Carried it, ripened it.
I thought, without a father there can be no child;
I took his side, my creator, not hers, my nurse.
In any case, your daughter –
I won't call her my mother –
Made . . . private bed-arrangements . . .
With another man. I blush to mention it –
Her shame is mine – but still:                                560
She had a private partner, here in the house,
Aigisthos. I killed him first, then her,
And so avenged my father.
Was I breaking the law, or keeping it?

You want me stoned for what I did.
I say it helped all Greece. What if
All wives took to murdering their husbands,
Baring their breasts to their children,
Begging for mercy – and getting away with it?
They'd kill their men for fun.
You call me an animal, but I put a stop to that.          570

I despised her, I killed her, and I was right –
A woman who kissed her man
Goodbye to the Trojan War
And ran straight to a lover's bed;
Knew what it meant, didn't blush,
Didn't kill herself when she was caught
But waited till he came home,
My father, killed him instead.
Ye gods – excuse me for bringing gods into this –
580   What else was I supposed to do? Keep quiet?
What would he have done, the victim?
He'd have cursed me, he'd be capering,
Here, now, with his Furies, his demons –
Or does only she have Furies?
Are there none for him, her victim?
It's your fault, grandfather. You destroyed me.
You fathered her. She was yours, that foulness
Who stole my father and made me murder her.
You've heard of Odysseus' wife, Penelope?
Her son doesn't murder her, and why? Because
590   She sleeps alone, no lovers stain her bed.
And what about Apollo?
At the navel of the earth he gives
Clear prophecies, not to be denied.
These orders were his.
He told me, 'Kill'; I killed –
So exile him, kill him,
The blame is his, not mine.
What else was I to do?
He ordered it; I did it;
If I can't trust him now,
Where else can I turn?
600   What was done was well done,
It turned out well – except for me who did it.
How happy they are whose marriages are happy.
How cursed they are,
What laughing-stocks they are,
Whose wives are whores.

**CHORUS.**
  It's women's fault. It's always been the same.
  When a man's in trouble, a woman is to blame.

**TYNDAREOS.**
  How dare you? Bluster, insolence,
  Smart answers to make me smart.
  I'll see you die for this. I'll enjoy it.        610
  I came to decorate my daughter's grave –
  And so I shall, by visiting the assembly
  And forcing them – they won't take much forcing –
  To have you stoned.
  Yes, and your sister beside you.
  She's earned it, filling your ears
  With tales about your mother,
  Prodding your hate. 'I dreamed of Agamemnon';
  'She's taken a lover' – God damn Aigisthos
  And all he's done to us! – day and night she made
  A bonfire of hate that engulfed this house.      620

  As for you, Menelaos, son-in-law, I warn you:
  I can make and I can break. Don't stand for him,
  Don't protect him and defy the gods,
  Let the townspeople stone him – or stay away
  From Sparta. You know your friends,
  Your enemies. That's all. I'm going. Slaves . . .

    *Exit.*

**ORESTES.**
  Thank heavens, old man!        630
  Now we can talk in peace.
  Menelaos, you're frowning,
  You're pacing. Why?

**MENELAOS.**
  I'm working it out.
  I'm puzzled.

**ORESTES.**
  There's more to be said.
  Hear that, then judge.

MENELAOS.
>There are times for words
>And times for silence. Speak.

ORESTES.
640   Long speeches cast long shadows.
>Menelaos, you owe me nothing,
>Except the one debt you owed my father.
>I don't mean money:
>Something more valuable,
>Life itself.
>I've done wrong. To cancel it
>You too must do wrong –
>Just as Agamemnon my father did wrong
>To gather troops and go to Troy
>To cancel the wrong
650   Your wife did here in Greece.
>He stood beside you, protected you
>As any brother would, till you won her back –
>Now you save me, your nephew.
>Ten years he gave you; one day is all I ask.

>As for Aulis, when he sacrificed
>My sister Iphigeneia to win fair sailing,
>I'll forget that, I won't demand life for life,
>Won't ask you kill
660   Hermione, your daughter. As things are now,
>I yield you that advantage. But yield me life,
>My own life, Elektra's life, for my father's sake,
>For this family's sake – we're all it has.

>You'll say, 'Impossible.' Of course –
>When the impossible comes, that's when we help
>Our friends, our family. When times are good,
>God helps us, we don't need family then.
>You love your wife, all Greece knows that.
670   I'm not making capital, not using that,
>But in her name I beg you – I'm ashamed
>To be brought to this! But what else can I do?
>I must, our whole future hangs on it –
>Majesty, uncle, these words are his, not mine,
>They come from your own dear brother,

Hovering, listening, begging.
I'm on my knees, tears in my eyes –
Have pity. All I ask
Is what all human beings ask: my life.

CHORUS.
    Hear him, lord.                                  680
    We're women, we're nothing,
    But we add our prayers to his.
    He needs you: help him.

MENELAOS.
    Orestes, I understand. I sympathise.
    For a kinsman, a brother's son,
    With God's good help
    We should do what we can, fight to the death –
    But that's the point: God has to help.
    I've been wandering for years;
    I've faced a thousand problems;
    My armies are gone,
    My spearmen, bowmen –                       690
    We're a handful. What hope have we
    Of defeating Argos by force of arms?
    Persuasion, diplomacy:
    They're what we need, they're essential.
    An angry mob, out of control,
    Is like a forest fire.
    If you haven't the strength,
    Don't tackle it head-on.
    Sit quietly by, let it rage and roar,
    Let it burn itself out, wait your moment,        700
    You'll get everything you want.
    Where there's passion, there'll be compassion –
    You'll get what you want if you bide your time.
    If you cram on all sail, you'll swamp the ship;
    If you slacken off, fair sailing.
    Don't fuss at the gods, don't push the mob.
    I'll go to them: Tyndareos, the people.
    I'll talk to them. Brains, not brawn.
    Soft soap, I won't deny it.                    710
    You expected armies, force of arms?

No chance. They're Argives,
They won't be beaten to their knees.
But subtle argument: that's what Fate demands,
That's what we'll use. No choice.

*Exit, attended.*

ORESTES.
Bastard. So hot for *her*, so eager
To fight for *her* – and then,
When it's flesh and blood, you slide away.
720    Your brother's house, Agamemnon's house!
Oh Father, who'll help us now? There's no one.
We're betrayed, we're dead. There's no way out.
We trusted Menelaos, and now we're dead.

Look: Pylades, running. My dearest friend,
All the way from Phokis. Thank God.
Smile, smile – a friend,
A trusted friend, calm after storm.

*Enter* PYLADES.

PYLADES.
Orestes, what's happening? I ran.
730    I saw a gang of them, I heard them,
Plotting to kill you, kill Elektra.
What is it? What's happening?
You're more than the world to me.

ORESTES.
I'm finished. That's all.

PYLADES.
If you die, I die. Friend, and friend.

ORESTES.
Menelaos has betrayed us.
Elektra and me: betrayed.

PYLADES.
What d'you expect?
Such a man, with such a wife!

ORESTES.
Why did he come?

What good was that to me?

PYLADES.
He's here? Here at last?

ORESTES.
After all these years. And at once – betrayal.  740

PYLADES.
And that wife of his, has he shipped her home?

ORESTES.
She crooked her finger, and home he came.

PYLADES.
That butcher of Greeks, where is she?

ORESTES.
Inside. In the palace:
My palace, if it *is* still mine.

PYLADES.
And Menelaos – Uncle Menelaos –
What did you ask him?

ORESTES.
Not to stand by and let them kill us.

PYLADES.
And what did he answer?

ORESTES.
Nothing definite. He said what traitors say.

PYLADES.
What, precisely? I don't understand.

ORESTES.
*He* came. The father of those daughters.  750

PYLADES.
Tyndareos. Not pleased about his daughter.

ORESTES.
Menelaos took his side, not my father's –

PYLADES.
And refused to fight for you?

ORESTES.
If I'd been a woman – he fights for them.

PYLADES.
So there's no hope? You're dead?

ORESTES.
It's a murder charge. They take a vote.

PYLADES.
What about? Tell me. You frighten me.

ORESTES.
Life, death. Short words, long shadows.

PYLADES.
For heaven's sake escape, then. Both of you.

ORESTES.
760    On every road, they've guards.

PYLADES.
I saw them. On every street, I saw them.

ORESTES.
We're like a city under siege.

PYLADES.
And *I've* troubles too. Ask me, I'll tell you.

ORESTES.
Troubles, like mine? What are they?

PYLADES.
I'm banished. By my own father.

ORESTES.
From home? From your city? Why?

PYLADES.
For helping you kill your mother.

ORESTES.
My fate taints you as well.

PYLADES.
I'm not Menelaos. I'll endure it.

ORESTES.
770    But why are you *here*? They'll kill you too.

PYLADES.
    I'm a citizen of Phokis. They can't touch me.

ORESTES.
    They're a rabble. Dogs led by dogs –

PYLADES.
    Not always. If lions lead them, lions.

ORESTES.
    That's it. *We'll* address them.

PYLADES.
    What will we say?

ORESTES.
    I'll put my case.

PYLADES.
    That you did what was right?

ORESTES.
    Avenging my father.

PYLADES.
    They'll tear you to pieces.

ORESTES.
    I'm to huddle here, and die?

PYLADES.
    I'm sorry.

ORESTES.
    So what should I do?

PYLADES.
    If you stay in Argos, you're dead?

ORESTES.
    Yes.

PYLADES.
    If you get away, there's hope?

ORESTES.
    If I'm lucky.

PYLADES.
    Going's better than staying?

780

ORESTES.
You want me to go.

PYLADES.
It's better than dying like a dog.

ORESTES.
To die bravely –

PYLADES.
You won't if you stay.

ORESTES.
My case is just.

PYLADES.
Let's find someone to think so –

ORESTES.
To take me in.

PYLADES.
After all – a prince.

ORESTES.
With a father to avenge.

PYLADES.
No question.

ORESTES.
Let's go, then. Not die like dogs.

PYLADES.
Well said.

ORESTES.
Shall we tell Elektra?

PYLADES.
Good God, no.

ORESTES.
She'd cry.

PYLADES.
Bad luck for certain.

ORESTES.
There is just one thing –

**PYLADES.**
  What?

**ORESTES.**
  If the goddesses come . . . another fit . . .

**PYLADES.**
  I'll see to you.

**ORESTES.**
  It's horrible.

**PYLADES.**
  I'll do it.

**ORESTES.**
  You could catch . . . what I've got.

**PYLADES.**
  For heaven's sake!

**ORESTES.**
  You don't mind?

**PYLADES.**
  I'm supposed to be your friend.

**ORESTES.**
  All right, let's go.

**PYLADES.**
  I'll help you.

**ORESTES.**
  First, to Father's grave.

**PYLADES.**
  What for?

**ORESTES.**
  I'll ask his protection.

**PYLADES.**
  He owes you a favour.

**ORESTES.**
  We won't go to Mother's grave.

**PYLADES.**
  Your enemy.

Be quick, before they cast their vote.
800 Lean on me . . . your weak side . . .
I'll support you through the town.
I don't mind. I'm your friend –
What better time than now to show it?

ORESTES.
'A friend in need', as the proverb says.
One such friend is worth ten thousand relatives.

*Exeunt. Music.*

CHORUS.
Prosperity, nobility,
High standing in Greece,
On the plains of Troy –
810 All gone. This house is cursed.
Golden lamb,
Murdered children,
Feasts of children's flesh,
Blood on blood,
Hand after hand after hand:
The house of Atreus.

Triumph no triumph, to slice her flesh,
Your mother, take blade
820 Forged in fire,
Lift it high, high,
Pearling with blood.
'She had to die' –
Delusion, crime.
She cried her own death.
'Don't kill me!
Crime after crime after crime:
830 He died; I die; you die.'

He's sick, he weeps,
All pain, all tears,
Blood hands, his mother's blood.
He did it, he did it!
He writhes, he groans,
Rolls white, red eyes.
They're after him,

Furies after him, Orestes!
She pulled back golden robe, 840
Bared breast, mother's breast –
He remembered his father, his father,
And cut her down.

*Music ends. Enter* ELEKTRA.

ELEKTRA.
Orestes. Where's Orestes?
Has he gone? Is he mad again?

CHORUS.
He's gone to the Assembly,
To face the people. They decide today,
For you, for him – are you to live or die?

ELEKTRA.
Oee moee. Who told him?

CHORUS.
Pylades. Someone's coming: look. 850
An old man, with news.

*Enter* OLD MAN.

OLD MAN.
Elektra, lady, princess, unhappy Elektra,
Disaster, hear me, disaster.

ELEKTRA.
Aee aee, we're dead. That's your news.
It's obvious: we're dead.

OLD MAN.
Dead, lady, your brother and yourself.
The vote's been taken.

ELEKTRA.
Oee moee. It's come. I dreaded it,
I wept, I cried, and now it's come. 860
What did they say, the people?
What arguments? And how are we to die?
Will they stone us, or cut our throats?

OLD MAN.
As it happened, I'd just come into town.

I'm a countryman, work in the fields.
I wanted to know what was happening,
To you and Orestes.
(I worked for your father once,
In the old days; your family looked after me;
I'm a poor man, but loyal.)
870   There was a crowd,
Climbing the hill where Danaos and Aigyptos,
Years ago, called a vote to settle that argument.
I asked someone,
'What is it? What's going on?
Some enemy approaching?'
*He* said, 'Look: Orestes. Over there.
Can't you see? His trial's today.'
He was right. I never expected to see
880   Such a sight, such a pitiful sight:
Orestes, Pylades,
Your brother tottering with sickness,
Pylades supporting him, helping him alone
As if *he* was his brother, or his nurse.

The rest of the people gathered. Silence.
'In the case of Orestes the matricide,
Who wants to speak?' Talthybios stood up –
He was with your father at the sack of Troy.
Sucking up to those in power, as usual.
He praised your father,
890   Didn't praise your brother,
Gave a cat's-cradle of arguments,
'Dangerous precedent' –
All the time fawning on Aigisthos' men.
A typical functionary:
No views of your own,
Choose the people in power
And lick their boots.

Diomedes was next, Lord Diomedes.
He wasn't for killing you, either of you;
900   Banishment, he said – far more appropriate.
Well, some of them cheered, and others booed.
Up jumps another one, a mouth on legs,

You know the type: loud, crude,
'A simple citizen' –
'Stone 'em,' he said,
'It's as simple as that: stone 'em.'
Your grandfather Tyndareos put him up to that.                910
Someone else stood up, said exactly the opposite.
No con-man this time, an honest face,
Not the kind who hangs around street corners,
A working man, a farmer, salt of the earth,                920
Decent, clean-living, listens to all the arguments
And then makes up his own mind. *He* said
Orestes, Lord Agamemnon's son, deserved
A medal for what he'd done, avenging his father,
Killing that bitch, hated by the gods, who'd tried
To steal all we had. Who'd go to war, he said,
Who'd ever leave home to fight,
If *that's* what happened to their wives?
A patter of applause: the family men.                930

No one else comes forward.
It's your brother's turn.
'People of Argos,' he says,
'It was for all of you,
Not just for my father,
That I killed my mother.
If we say it's legal
For wives to kill their husbands,
Which man of us is safe?
We'd be in their hands.
Don't do it. She betrayed my father,
And died for it. If you kill me now,                940
The law stands on its head,
They'll do as they like, you're all as good as dead.'

Fine words, but they weren't about to listen.
The loudmouth was shouting, 'Death!'
A show of hands. He won.
Orestes – what could he do? – persuaded them
To put down their stones.
'By my own hand I'll die,' he said.
'Elektra, too.' The Assembly's done.

950   They're coming: your brother, Pylades,
      In tears, their supporters, weeping and mourning.
      A sad sight.
      Prepare yourself lady:
      Knife, noose, you must.
      Granddaughter of Atreus!
      What use is that to you?
      It's Apollo, Phoebus Apollo — he's to blame.

      *Exit. Music.*

CHORUS.
960   Weep, Argos, weep with us.
      Sharp nails, white cheeks, blood-furrows.
      Beat head, for her, for her,
      Persephone, who rules the Dead below.
      Weep, Argos, weep with us.
      Sharp knife, chopped hair, shorn head.
      Weep for them, weep, who once
970   Led Greece to war, and now must die.

      Gone, now, forever gone,
      That famous house of Atreus,
      Once blessed, now cursed by God,
      Cursed by the people, whose vote is death.
      Eeoh, eeoh, forever gone,
      We live, we hope, we die.
980   Fate rules our lives, our lives,
      We're mortal, live little lives, and die.

ELEKTRA.
      There, lift me there,
      Space-vault on high
      Where the boulder torn,
      Whirlwind-torn,
      From Olympos torn,
      Floats on golden chains.
      I'll cry to him there,
      To Tantalos, who made us, sired us,
      I'll cry how the curse began.
      It began with Pelops, riding, flying,
      Racing chariot on smooth white sand,

White sand by foaming sea —
And Myrtilos,
Crashing,
Drowning,
Dying.                                           990
On it came,
Curse, tears,
Ram with golden fleece
In his flocks,
In Hermes' flocks,
Destruction for Atreus, horselord.               1000
War then,
War changed the sky,
Sun reeled,
Dawn's horses,
White horses, bolted,
Lord Zeus reversed the sky.
Still it spreads,
Curse,
Stain,
Death on death:
Thyestes' unholy feast,                          1010
Adulterous Airope,
My brother, myself,
Fate, pain, despair.

*Music ends.*

CHORUS.
He's coming, your brother
Condemned to die, and Pylades
Truest of friends, a brother,
Supporting him, helping him.

*Enter* ORESTES *and* PYLADES.

ELEKTRA.
Oee goh, Orestes, so near to death, the grave.
Oee goh, how can I bear it? How?                 1020

ORESTES.
Be quiet. Woman's wailing! It's decided:
Put up with it. It can't be helped.

ELEKTRA.
How can I be quiet? The sun,
We're condemned, they'll snatch us from the sun.

ORESTES.
I'm condemned to death: that's bad enough.
Now you're killing me twice over. Be quiet.

ELEKTRA.
Darling boy, poor boy. To die so young.
1030    You should be alive, not dead, alive.

ORESTES.
In God's name! Weeping and wailing –
You'll have me at it. Am I to break down too?

ELEKTRA.
We're to die. How can't I weep?
They're snatching our lives, our lovely lives.

ORESTES.
It's decided. Today. Sword or stones:
It's for us to choose.

ELEKTRA.
Orestes, *you* kill me, *you*, not them.
Agamemnon's daughter!
Don't let some Argive shame me.

ORESTES.
I've our mother's blood already on my hands.
I won't have yours as well. Do it yourself;
1040    Choose how.

ELEKTRA.
With a sword. Your sword. Like you.
But first, first, let me hug you, kiss you.

ORESTES.
What good will it do,
Hugging, kissing at the door of death?
Still, if you must –

ELEKTRA.
Darling, dearest, my only love,
My body, my breath of life.

ORESTES.
> I can't bear it. She wants me to hold her.
> I must. Why not? I'm not ashamed.
> Sister, darling, precious, hold me,
> Marriage, children, hug me, this is all we have.      1050

ELEKTRA.
> Feoo.
> If only one sword could kill us both,
> One grave receive us both . . .

ORESTES.
> If only . . . But there's no one, no one left alive,
> No kinsman left, to bury us.

ELEKTRA.
> Menelaos spoke up for you, spoke for your life –
> Didn't he? The traitor. The coward.
> He didn't speak, for Father's sake?

ORESTES.
> He wasn't even there. He wants the crown;
> We're in his way; he won't save us.
> We're Agamemnon's children: it's up to us      1060
> To honour him, die nobly,
> Die as his children should,
> Show Argos who we are. I'll fall on my sword,
> Then you . . . do the same, do the same, be brave.
> Pylades, watch and wait. As soon as we're dead,
> Lay out our bodies, bury us together, there
> By Father's grave. It's time. Farewell.

PYLADES.
> Wait. How dare you?
> You'll kill yourself, and think I want to live?      1070

ORESTES.
> I have to die. But why should you?

PYLADES.
> How can you ask? You're my friend: I love you.

ORESTES.
> You didn't kill your mother. I killed mine.

PYLADES.
    I helped, I was there. I share the guilt.

ORESTES.
    You've a father to live for,
    A native land, a people, a palace, wealth.
    All mine are gone.
    You won't marry Elektra,
    As once I promised you –
    But find someone else,
1080    Find happiness, children.
    We'd have been brothers. No more.
    Farewell, dear friend, farewell.
    She and I: we're dead.
    How can we fare well?

PYLADES.
    You don't understand.
    May the fruitful earth not drink my blood,
    May bright air not receive my soul,
    If I betray you, if I abandon you now,
    Shake free of you. I killed with you,
1090    We planned it, did it together.
    I'm proud of it, and proud to die with you –
    Both of you: my friend, my promised wife.
    If I went home now, what would I say
    To my people, high in Phokis –
    'I was his friend, while things went well;
    When disaster came, I left'? We share to the end –
    And before that end, before we die,
    Let's find a way to break Menelaos' heart.

ORESTES.
1100    To do that, see that, is to die content.

PYLADES.
    Wait then. Sheathe your sword, for now.

ORESTES.
    To take revenge on the man I hate . . .

PYLADES.
    Shh! These women. I don't trust women.

ORESTES.
  It's all right. They're ours. They're on our side.

PYLADES.
  Well then. Break Menelaos' heart. Kill Helen –

ORESTES.
  How? I'm ready, eager – but how?

PYLADES.
  Cut her throat. Is she there inside?

ORESTES.
  She's making lists – of my father's treasures.

PYLADES.
  Not any more. She has a date, in Hell.

ORESTES.
  But how? She has servants, Trojans.                    1110

PYLADES.
  Foreign riffraff? They don't scare me.

ORESTES.
  Mirror-bearers, perfume-dabbers –

PYLADES.
  She's brought them *with* her?

ORESTES.
  She finds us Greeks 'provincial'.

PYLADES.
  They're slaves. Won't fight free men.

ORESTES.
  If we bring this off, they can kill me twice.

PYLADES.
  If I die at your side, they can kill me too.

ORESTES.
  How shall we do it?

PYLADES.
  We'll say we're going to kill ourselves . . . go in . . .

ORESTES.
  Then what?                                             1120

PYLADES.
We'll go to her, we'll cry and moan . . .

ORESTES.
She'll cry with us. But inside, she'll laugh.

PYLADES.
And so will we.

ORESTES.
What next?

PYLADES.
Knives, hidden in our clothes.

ORESTES.
But what about the slaves?

PYLADES.
We'll lock them out –

ORESTES.
And if they shout, they're dead.

PYLADES.
The rest is easy.

ORESTES.
1130  Cut Helen's throat.

PYLADES.
Precisely. It's foolproof.
If we were murdering some *honest* woman,
That would be a crime. But Helen!
She owes the whole of Greece her death.
All those whose fathers, husbands, children, died
For her – they'll cheer, light bonfires of celebration,
They'll fall on their knees and beg the gods
To shower us with blessings, you and me,
1140  Bitch-killers. 'Matricide', they call you –
No more of that, 'Helenicide' they'll call you now,
Fall on your neck.
Why should Menelaos have life, have luck,
While you all die, your father, your sister, you,
Your mother? No, not her, forget I said that.
Agamemnon's army wins him back his wife,

And he grabs Agamemnon's throne?
Oh no, I'll lift this sword and slice her,
Or die in the attempt.                                    1150
And if we can't get near her,
We'll burn the palace
To make our own funeral pyre.
An honourable death
Or a glorious deliverance – how can we fail?

CHORUS.
She deserves it, Tyndareos' daughter,
Despised by all women: she's soiled her sex.

ORESTES.
Feoo.
What better than a friend,
A real friend? Not gold, not power –
Give me one good friend, and keep them all.
You planned that big surprise for Aigisthos,
Stood by me when trouble came,
And now you give me revenge on those I hate,   1160
You don't run away – I won't go on,
It's embarrassing, I'll spare your blushes.
I'm doomed to die, but before I go
I want to hurt that traitor, that betrayer,
Make him weep as he made me weep.
My father was Agamemnon,
Grand Admiral of Greece – by merit,
Not by inheritance, by God's good grace.
What, shall I die like a slave, disgrace him?    1170
No! I'll die of my own free choice,
Make Menelaos pay. Unless . . . what if . . .
If God would just grant that . . .
Suppose we killed, and escaped alive?
God hear me. Hope? I pray for it,
Words fly on the wind, and lift the soul.

ELEKTRA.
Orestes, I know a way: to kill, and escape alive,
You, me, Pylades, all three of us.

ORESTES.
God's helping us, you mean? Or what?
1180   You've some plan, some cunning plan?

ELEKTRA.
Listen. Pylades, you too.

ORESTES.
Tell me. Good news to make me smile.

ELEKTRA.
You know she has a daughter?
Of course you do.

ORESTES.
Hermione, yes.
Our mother brought her up.

ELEKTRA.
She's gone to our mother's grave –

ORESTES.
What for? What's that to us?

ELEKTRA.
Helen sent her, with offerings.

ORESTES.
How does that help us?

ELEKTRA.
When she comes back, grab her. Hostage.

ORESTES.
1190   I still don't understand.

ELEKTRA.
When Helen's dead, if Menelaos tries anything –
Against you, me, Pylades, any of us –
Tell him we'll kill Hermione.
Hold your knife to her throat.
If he agrees to let you go, to save her life,
Even though Helen's swimming in blood,
There at his feet, give her back to him.
If he rages and roars for vengeance,
1200   Lift the knife. He'll soon change his mind.
Sound and fury; underneath, he's soft.

That's the plan. It'll save us all. That's it.

ORESTES.
You . . . man!
Woman's looks, man's brain –
Pylades, this is the wife you stand to lose,
Or win, if all goes well, if we all survive.

PYLADES.
If only. I hear the wedding-songs already,
The bridal procession, the people singing –          1210

ORESTES.
Where *is* Hermione? How soon will she be here?
To net that traitor's cub – it's brilliant.

ELEKTRA.
She'll be here any moment. She's had time enough.
She's coming. It's now, it's now.

ORESTES.
All right. Elektra, you stay out here,
Greet her when she comes.
And keep good watch while the killing happens.
If anyone comes – Menelaos, one of his servants,
Knock on the door or call some warning.          1220
Pylades, it's now. Hands on knives. Inside.

  *Music.*

Agamemnon, Father,
Asleep in the folds of dark,
Hear me, Orestes.
I killed for you;
I was condemned for you;
Your brother deserted me,
And now I mean to make him pay.
Agamemnon, hear me,
Hear and help.          1230

ELEKTRA.
Father, hear us,
Deep in the Underworld,
Hear us, your children,
Calling you, dying for you.

PYLADES.
Agamemnon, father-in-law,
Hear me: save your son, your daughter.

ORESTES.
I killed my mother.

ELEKTRA.
I armed him.

PYLADES.
I urged him.

ORESTES.
Father, for you.

ELEKTRA.
For you.

PYLADES.
Hear them, help them.

ORESTES.
With tears we pray —

ELEKTRA.
We offer tears.

*Music ends.*

PYLADES.
1240   Right. If prayers penetrate the earth, he hears.
It's time. Father Zeus,
Justice who rules on high,
Send us success, Orestes, Elektra, Pylades.
Three allies, a single test, a single judgement:
One for all, all for one, for life or death!

*Exeunt* ORESTES *and* PYLADES. *Music.*

ELEKTRA.
Women of Argos, friends,
Ladies of high degree —

CHORUS.
Elektra, princess, what?
1250   Princess, till the day you die.

ELEKTRA.
>Watch with me, watch.
>Some here, some there.

CHORUS.
>Why? Why?

ELEKTRA.
>In case they come, someone comes
>And stumbles on the deed of blood,
>New pain on old.

CHORUS A.
>We'll watch this side,
>Where sun slants, east.

CHORUS B.
>We'll watch this side,
>Where sun sinks, west.                          1260

ELEKTRA.
>Close watch. This side,
>That side, close watch.

CHORUS.
>We watch, we watch.

ELEKTRA.
>Keep careful watch, keep watch,
>Keen eyes, eyes open, watch.

CHORUS A.
>Look! Someone's coming. There.
>A farmer, by the palace wall.                   1270

ELEKTRA.
>We're done for, friends.
>He'll tell. He'll tell.

CHORUS A.
>He's gone.

ELEKTRA.
>The other side? Still clear?
>There's no one there? The courtyard's clear?
>Tell me. Oh tell.

CHORUS B.
> There's no one here.
> Keep watch that side.

CHORUS A.
> We are, we are.
1280 > There's no one here.

ELEKTRA.
> I'll call them. Here.
> Mouth to the door.
> (*Calling.*) What's happening?
> There's no one.
> Do it! Do it!
>
> No answer. We're dead.
> Their knives blunt at her beauty.
> They're coming, Argives,
1290 > Running to save her.
> Look again. Change sides.
> Don't stand. Change sides.

CHORUS A.
> I'm here.

CHORUS B.
> I'm here.

HELEN (*inside*).
> Eeoh, help me, murder, help.

ELEKTRA.
> Did you hear? It's murder.

CHORUS.
> Helen's voice, perhaps?

ELEKTRA.
> Zeus, Zeus above,
1300 > Protect them now.

HELEN (*inside*).
> Menelaos. Where are you? Help me!

ELEKTRA *and* CHORUS.
> Kill, stab, slice,
> Knives bite, swords bite.

Whore-Helen,
Killer, corpse-maker,
Thousands died for you,
Tears, blood, tears,
Red water, river-water, red,
Running red with blood.                                    1310

CHORUS.
Sh! Someone's coming.
There, beside the wall.

*Music ends.*

ELEKTRA.
Friends, it's Hermione –
Right in the middle of the murder.
Sh!
She's walking into the net.
What a pretty catch, if only we catch her.
Back on guard. Look natural!
Like me, look. Eyes downcast.
Nothing's happening.                                       1320

*Enter* HERMIONE.

Hermione. Sweetheart.
Have you been to the grave?
Have you poured your offerings
To . . . her below?

HERMIONE.
Yes. I'm sure she was pleased.
What's happening?
I heard shouting, inside.
All the way down the road.
I'm frightened.

ELEKTRA.
Of course you did.
Of course we were shouting.

HERMIONE.
God help you. Why were you shouting?

ELEKTRA.
Orestes and I – we're to die today.

HERMIONE.
Elektra, no! Not you! Not Orestes!

ELEKTRA.
1330 It's decided. What must happen, must happen.

HERMIONE.
Is that why there's shouting. . . ?

ELEKTRA.
Oh yes. He went straight to Helen.

HERMIONE.
Who did? Tell me! I don't understand.

ELEKTRA.
Orestes. Went to her. So we wouldn't die.

HERMIONE.
That's why there's all that noise.

ELEKTRA.
What else should there be noise about?
They're inside, your cousins, touching her heart.
1340 Go in, sweetheart, beg her ladyship
To pity us, help us. We need you now, inside.
Come on, I'll take you.

HERMIONE.
Let's run. If it's up to me, you're safe.

ELEKTRA (*at the door*).
Orestes, Pylades, draw your swords.
The quarry's here. It's now!

HERMIONE (*at the door*).
Oee goh. Who are you?

ORESTES.
Never mind. We're here to save us, not you.

ELEKTRA.
1350 Grab her. Knife to the throat. Not a sound.
Show Menelaos it's men he's dealing with,
Not cowards from Troy. Go to his heart.

*She follows* HERMIONE *inside. Noise inside.
Music.*

CHORUS.
>Eeoh, eeoh,
>Stamp, dance, sing
>Here, outside.
>They mustn't hear,
>Mustn't run to help,
>Till we see her drowned in blood,
>Till they tell us she's dead, she's dead:          1360
>Helen, cursed of the gods,
>Who filled all Greece with tears,
>Who slept with Paris, with Paris,
>And took all Greece to Troy.

>The door. Someone's opening the door.
>Someone's coming: a slave, a Trojan.
>Now we'll know what's happening, inside.

>*Enter* TROJAN.

TROJAN.
>They're hunting me. Greeks, hunting me.
>Greek knives.
>Out I slip, I climb,                               1370
>My slippers on the roof, I jump.
>Troy's gone, my city's gone,
>Why should I hide?
>Aee aee.
>Where now, friends, now?
>Shall I fly in the sky, the fleecy sky,
>Or swim the sea, bull-sea
>That swarms, that clutches earth?

CHORUS.
>One of Helen's slaves. What is it?                 1380

TROJAN.
>Oh moee moee, Troy, Troy,
>City walls, green hills, I weep for you,
>You're gone, Troy's gone, I weep oh weep.
>She did it, Leda's brat,
>Swan-white, swan-feathered,
>Helen Hell-to-Men.
>She broke, she crushed,

My city's crushed, otototo toee,
1390 yal-EH-mohn, yal-EH-mohn,
Troy's loveliness, destroyed.

**CHORUS.**
Start again. What's happening, inside?

**TROJAN.**
AI-li-non, AI-li-non, aee, aee,
Tears, death,
Aee, aee, royal blood,
Hell-knives stab, earth drinks.
1400 They came (I tell you all):
Two lions, Greek lions –
Orestes, his lordship's son;
Pylades, who cheats in dark,
Fast-fighting,
Snake, I spit on him.
They came. She sat,
Paris' wife,
1410 Paris arrowlord.
Tears fouled their eyes.
They knelt:
This side, that side,
Humbly, like slaves.
Hugged close her legs.
Up we ran,
We slaves, we Trojans –
Who knew what was happening?
1420 'Nothing's wrong.' 'It's a trick.'
'They're snaring her:
He's netting her, snaring her,
The son, the mother-killer, monster.'

**CHORUS.**
And you?
Where exactly were you?
You'd run away?

**TROJAN.**
In Troy, in Troy,
We had fans, feather-fans,

Slaves to waft them, I was there,
Cooling, cooling my lady's cheeks.
She was spinning –
A golden distaff,                                          1430
Spinning, spoils of Troy –
Purple threads,
Grave-gifts, for Klytemnestra's grave.
Orestes said,
'Majesty, down,
Step down from the throne,
Come to the altar-hearth,
Hear what I have to say.'                                  1440
He led the way,
She followed,
Guessed nothing of his plans.
The other one,
That man from Phokis,
He turned on us:
'Out, scum, Trojan scum,
Out of the way, get out!'
We ran, and he locked us where we ran:
In the stables, the barns, anywhere                        1450
Away from our lady, far away.

CHORUS.
  And then? What then?

TROJAN.
  id-a-EE-a-MAH-ter, MAH-ter,
  Blood, murder, I saw it,
  There in the palace, saw it.
  Knives they had, knives in their sleeves.
  They looked this way, that way: no one.
  They hurtled on her, boars,                              1460
  Like mountain boars, charging.
  'Die!' they shouted, 'Die!
  It's Menelaos' fault, he betrayed us,
  You die for him, you die.'
  My lady was screaming, 'Oh moee moee',
  White arms beat breast,
  Beat head, she ran,

Dropped golden sandal, fell.
Orestes grabbed her hair,
1470    Put his boot on her neck, bent it back,
Took his knife, blue knife, to cut her throat.

CHORUS.
Didn't you help her?
The palace, full of slaves —
Did no one help her?

TROJAN.
We yelled, fetched crowbars,
Broke the doors,
Smashed doorframes,
Ran to help her, ran.
Some had stones, some slings, some swords.
Pylades stood there, terrible,
A warrior, an Aias —
I saw them at the gates
1480    When they killed our Troy.
We fought. Blades rang.
But what could we do?
We were Trojans, he was Greek.
We ran, we hid,
We begged for our lives,
We died. Dead in the dark,
We died. Then *she* came:
Hermione, poor Hermione.
1490    Her mother was fainting, falling.
Orestes and Pylades ran, pounced on her,
Grabbed her. And when they turned back
My lady was gone: she'd disappeared, thin air.
Zeus, Mother Earth, Light, Dark,
What magic was here, what spell, what god?
What happened next? I don't know.
I picked up my legs and ran.
1500    Disaster, disaster,
Menelaos fetched her home from Troy
For this, for this!

CHORUS.
Something else. Orestes is coming,

Hurrying, sword in hand. He's here.

*Enter* ORESTES. *Music ends.*

ORESTES.
Where is he?
He dodged, he ran.
Where is he?

TROJAN.
Lord, master, I bow, I hug the ground –

ORESTES.
Get up. This is Greece, not Troy.

TROJAN.
Even here, let me live, not die.

ORESTES.
You've been shouting for help.                                    1510
'Help! Menelaos! Help!'

TROJAN.
No, lord. You're my master, I shout for you.

ORESTES.
That woman deserved to die?

TROJAN.
Die, yes. If she had three necks,
Three lives – all die.

ORESTES.
You're lying. You're terrified.

TROJAN.
I mean it. She killed all Greece, all Troy.

ORESTES.
Swear, or die. You're saying what I want to hear.

TROJAN.
I'm not. On my life I swear.

ORESTES.
Was it like this in Troy?
Were you scared of . . . this?

TROJAN.
Take it away. It gleams. Death gleams.

ORESTES.
1520   It frightens you. It's a Gorgon's head.

TROJAN.
I see my death, no Gorgon.

ORESTES.
You're a slave, death frees you – and you're afraid?

TROJAN.
Free people, slaves, all love their life.

ORESTES.
Well said. You can live. Go in.

TROJAN.
You'll spare my life?

ORESTES.
Yes.

TROJAN.
It's good.

ORESTES.
But wait a minute –

TROJAN.
It's not good.

ORESTES.
Don't be silly. I don't want your throat –
You're a coward, not a man, not a woman.
I came out here to shut you up,
1530   Stop you raising a hue-and-cry. Menelaos:
He's the one I want. Those long, red curls.
Get him here. And if he comes in arms,
Comes with soldiers to storm the palace,
Refuses to set me free, and Pylades, and Elektra,
He'll see his daughter dead to join his wife.

*Exit* TROJAN. ORESTES *goes in. Music.*

CHORUS.
Eeoh, eeoh,
Tears, doom, pain,
Disaster.
Shall we tell the town?

Shall we stay where we are?                                    1540
Stay here, stay here.
Smoke, plumes of smoke
Tell their message, high in the air:
They're burning the palace,
The house of Atreus:
God's will, revenge
For long-past, ancient wrongs.

   *Music ends.*

Menelaos, running. They've told him.                           1550
– Bolt the doors, quickly.
– Orestes, he's up, you're down: be careful.

   *Enter* MENELAOS, *attended.*

MENELAOS.
   What's going on? Two wild beasts, they say –
   I won't call them men – raging in the palace.
   And Her Majesty . . . they say
   She's disappeared, not dead.
   The man was babbling, a fool, babbling with fear –
   No, it's a trick, it's that mother-murderer.
   Open up!
   You men, force the doors.                                   1560
   Find those murderers,
   Find my daughter, rescue her –
   And Her Majesty, find her
   Or kill the man who murdered her.

   ORESTES *and* PYLADES *appear on the roof,*
   *with* HERMIONE.

ORESTES.
   You. Don't touch that door.
   Menelaos, I mean, Sir Arrogance.
   You see these battlements?
   They're old, loose stones.                                  1570
   Make one false move, watch out for your skull.
   The doors are barred and bolted.
   Huff and puff all you like,
   You won't get in.

MENELAOS.
>   Who are you? Up there? Torches . . . smoke . . .
>   Who's that on the roof?
>   Who's holding my daughter?
>   Whose knife at her throat?

ORESTES.
>   Are you going to ask questions all night,
>   Or listen?

MENELAOS.
>   Do I have a choice? I'll listen.

ORESTES.
>   Then, first:
>   I'm the man who's going to kill your daughter.

MENELAOS.
>   You murdered Helen, and now you'll murder her?

ORESTES.
1580 >   Not Helen, no. God cheated me of that.

MENELAOS.
>   She's still alive? You're lying.

ORESTES.
>   If only I was. If only I'd –

MENELAOS.
>   Done what? Tell me!

ORESTES.
>   Sent that butcher of Greeks where she belongs.

MENELAOS.
>   Your mother's blood not enough for you?

ORESTES.
>   While there are whores in Greece to kill, I'll kill.

MENELAOS.
>   Give me Helen's body, to bury her.

ORESTES.
>   Go ask the gods. I'll kill this one too.

MENELAOS.
>   Mother-murderer. You've got the taste for it.

ORESTES.
  Father-avenger. My father, whom you betrayed.      1590

MENELAOS.
  Pylades, are you involved in this?

ORESTES.
  Of course he is. I speak for him.

MENELAOS.
  You'll suffer. Unless you mean to fly away.

ORESTES.
  We won't fly. We'll burn the palace.

MENELAOS.
  Your father's palace?

ORESTES.
  We'll burn it, and throw *her* on the flames.

MENELAOS.
  Kill her, and suffer.

ORESTES.
  As you wish.

MENELAOS.
  Ah! Ah! No! Stop!

ORESTES.
  Shut up, then, and listen. You've asked for this.

MENELAOS.
  You demand your life?

ORESTES.
  And my kingdom.                                           1600

MENELAOS.
  What kingdom?

ORESTES.
  This one. Argos.

MENELAOS.
  You'd sacrifice to Argos' gods?

ORESTES.
  Why not?

MENELAOS.
  Touch holy vessels – you?

ORESTES.
  Who else d'you suggest – yourself?

MENELAOS.
  My hands are clean.

ORESTES.
  But not your heart.

MENELAOS.
  Who'd speak to you?

ORESTES.
  Those who respect their fathers.

MENELAOS.
  And those who respect their mothers?

ORESTES.
  They're lucky.

MENELAOS.
  Luckier than you.

ORESTES.
  I despise all whores.

MENELAOS.
  So spare my daughter.

ORESTES.
  I don't trust you.

MENELAOS.
  So you'll kill her?

ORESTES.
  Precisely.

MENELAOS.
  Oee moee. What am I to do?

ORESTES.
1610   Go to the people. Tell them.

MENELAOS.
  Tell them what?

ORESTES.
Our lives must be spared –

MENELAOS.
– or you'll kill my child?

ORESTES.
Exactly.

MENELAOS.
Poor Helen . . .

ORESTES.
Poor Helen? Poor Orestes!

MENELAOS.
I brought you from Troy – to die!

ORESTES.
If only you had.

MENELAOS.
I worked so hard.

ORESTES.
But not for me.

MENELAOS.
It's outrageous.

ORESTES.
You had the choice.

MENELAOS.
I'm trapped.

ORESTES.
You trapped yourself. Your choice.
Elektra, light the fire below. Pylades, up here.          1620

MENELAOS.
People of Argos, where are you?
Help me! He murdered his mother,
Polluted your city – and wants to live!

   *Melée.* APOLLO *and* HELEN *appear on high.*

APOLLO.
Menelaos, blunt your fury.
Apollo speaks.

Orestes, put down your knife.
God's words.
First, for Helen.
You were hot for her blood,
1630   Hot to kill her to spite Menelaos –
And you failed. She's here,
She's safe, Zeus' daughter,
At Heaven's gate. Zeus ordered it.
Eternal life is hers:
With Kastor and Polydeukes,
Her brothers, she'll sit
Enthroned in the sky-vault,
A mark for sailors.
Her beauty was our instrument,
God's instrument,
To set Greeks and Trojans
1640   At one another's throats,
To glut the world with death,
To cull the human race.
She's ours.
Menelaos, take another mortal wife.

Orestes, next.
Go from Argos to Arkadia.
Live there, one year,
Then stand your trial in Athens.
The charge: matricide.
1650   The accusers: your mother's Furies.
Your place of trial: the Areiopagos.
Your judges: gods.
The trial will be fair; you'll win.
And as for her, Hermione,
The child you threaten:
One day you'll marry her.
Neoptolemos, Achilles' son,
Has hopes for her,
But he'll die before he marries her –
At Delphi,
Where he'll come to pray to me,
For the justice due his father.

Marry Elektra to Pylades,
As you said you would:
They'll find their happiness.

So it stands, Menelaos.
Leave Orestes to rule in Argos.                    1660
I'll speak for him to the people.
I ordered his mother's death.
Go home to Sparta, rule in peace.
This is Helen's dowry,
After years of bitterness:
A quiet life at last.

ORESTES.
Lord Apollo, I was afraid before,
That the voices I heard in your shrine,
Your orders, were demons from other worlds.
Now I know they were true. I hear and obey:   1670
Hermione's free. Menelaos, I ask her hand.

MENELAOS.
Helen, Zeus-born, farewell. You share
The gods' eternal happiness: I envy you.
As for you, Orestes: I hear Apollo's words,
I, too, hear and obey. Marry my daughter,
Be happy, two royal lines united.

APOLLO.
Your destinies are clear. Your quarrel's done.

MENELAOS.
As my Lord requires.

ORESTES.
As my Lord requires:                              1680
Peace now, forever, as the gods ordain.

APOLLO.
Go now, each go your way.
Bless lovely Peace. And I
With Helen, hand in hand,
Through fields of stars
To Heaven's bright halls above.
There, next to Hera's throne,

Her place forever fixed,
For sailors a shining light,
1690   Queen of the restless sea.

*Music.*

CHORUS.
Victory, lady,
Smile on me, forever,
Crown me.

*Exeunt.*

# IPHIGENEIA IN TAURIS

*translated by Kenneth McLeish*

# Characters

IPHIGENEIA
ORESTES
PYLADES
HERDSMAN
THOAS
ATTENDANT
ATHENE
GUARDS, ATTENDANTS (non-speaking)
CHORUS OF GREEK WOMEN, prisoners-of-war

*The sacred area outside a temple of Artemis on the
Crimean coast. There is an altar, bloodstained. Enter*
IPHIGENEIA.


IPHIGENEIA.
My great-grandfather was Pelops.
He galloped to Pisa
And married my great-grandmother.
Their son was Atreus.
His children were Menelaos, my uncle,
And Agamemnon, my father.
Klytemnestra my mother.
My name: Iphigeneia,
I'm the one my father sacrificed,
Far from here, in Greece, in a bay called Aulis –
You must have heard of it –
Where winds sweep currents, dark currents,
To and fro . . . That's right, sacrificed me,
For Helen, or so people thought.
You remember the story. A thousand ships,                    10
From every state in Greece, gathered in Aulis,
To sail for Troy, topple Troy,
Fetch Helen back, Menelaos' wife
Who'd been stolen by Prince Paris;
A thousand ships, commanded by my father,
Agamemnon, Grand Admiral of Greece –
And the gods held back the winds.
Agamemnon made sacrifice, asked what to do,
And the prophet said, 'Majesty,
Warlord of Greece, you made a vow, years ago,
To Artemis: you'd sacrifice to her
The most beautiful thing in Argos.
Well, that most beautiful thing
Is your daughter, Iphigeneia,
Your own and Klytemnestra's daughter.
If you want winds for your ships,
Take her, sacrifice her,
Blood for the goddess. Your own hand: do it.'          20

So they sent for me:

Odysseus invented a story,
That I was to marry Achilles.
They took me from my mother.
I went to Aulis. They held me.
The altar fire. My father's knife –
And just as the blow fell
Artemis spirited me away.
She gave them a deer, they killed a deer,
They thought it was Agamemnon's child.
As for me, through thin air she brought me here.
30    It's nowhere. Savages live here.
They've a clan-chief, Thoas, another savage.
I call him Thoas, you understand:
That's his Greek name. It means 'Speedy':
He runs fast.
Our Lady Artemis made me priestess here.
At all her rites I officiate. Grim rites,
A grim mistress. I do as I'm told.
What are they? When Greeks land here,
I offer them – not in person, you understand,
40    I don't lift the knife myself, others do that,
Inside. Blood-sacrifice, silent, terrible.

All night, now, dreams. Nightmares.
I had to come outside, tell the sky, find ease.
I'd escaped, I was home in Argos,
My women beside me. Sleeping.
All at once, an earthquake.
The whole ground writhed. I ran outside,
I watched the palace collapse in rubble.
Roof, walls, rubble. And in the midst of it all,
In all that was left of my father's house,
50    One pillar stood tall and safe.
Blond hair, human voice.
And what did I do for it?
What I do for all Greeks:
I wept, poured water, the ritual of death.
It means Orestes: my father's son,
My brother. Sons are pillars of the house,
We call them that. Orestes is dead,

I must weep for him, the ritual of death.
That's what it meant, the dream –
But he isn't here, he's far away, in Phokis.                    60
I'll go inside. I'll pray for him;
My women will pray for him,
The ones his barbarian Majesty
Found for me in Greece. Where are they?
They should be here. I'll go inside:
In our Lady's temple, I'll pray for him.

*Exit. Enter* ORESTES *and* PYLADES.

ORESTES.
Pylades! Down! There may be guards.

PYLADES.
Orestes, I've looked. There's no one.

ORESTES.
D'you think this is it? This is the temple
We sailed all this way to find?                                70

PYLADES.
Where else should it be?

ORESTES.
Look, on the altar: blood. Greek blood.

PYLADES.
Dreadlocks of blood.

ORESTES.
Shields, hanging on the wall.

PYLADES.
Their victims' shields.
Orestes, stay here. I'll check it's clear.

ORESTES.
It's a trap, Apollo, another trap. Why?
I did everything you told me:
I avenged my father, killed my mother,
And I'm an exile, driven out of Greece.
Furies haunt me, bloodhounds,
They hunt me, no rest, whirling, whirling.                      80
I came to you, I asked you: end it,

Whirling, Orestes the mad one,
End it, whirling, throughout all Greece.
'Go to the ends of the earth,' you said.
'Go to our Lady's shrine,
Our Lady Artemis, Apollo's sister. Go.
Her statue fell from the sky, they say:
90    Find a way to steal it, take it to Athens,
Present it to the people.' Just like that.
'It'll ease your pain,' you said;
'You'll be free at last,' you said.
Well, I'm here, at the ends of the earth.
I'm here, and there's no one. Now what?

Pylades, help me. It's what you came for.
How do we get inside? Climb the walls?
Look how high they are.
Use ladders? They'd see us.
Force the doors, use crowbars,
Break the bolts? We can't risk it:
100    They'd hear us, they'd kill us.
It's hopeless. Back to the ship.
They'll find us. It's hopeless.

PYLADES.
One thing's sure: we won't be running.
Princes don't run. God sent us here,
We can't avoid it. We'll hide.
There are caves, down by the shore,
Curtained by spray, away from the ship –
Someone's bound to see it, tell the authorities,
And we don't want them to find us.
110    Then, tonight,
When sky shuts its eyes,
We'll slip inside,
Find the statue, somehow –
It's polished wood, it gleams –
Steal it. Look, up there,
In the eaves: we can get in there.
Brave men succeed; cowards always fail.
We haven't rowed all this way for nothing.
Row back empty-handed? Not us, not us.

ORESTES.
  You're right. We'll do it. Apollo ordered it –
  He can't give orders and then prevent them.
  Nothing ventured, nothing won: we'll do it.

  *Exeunt. Music. Enter* CHORUS.

CHORUS.
  Respect us,
  Servants of the goddess.
  People of these cliffs, these shores,
  Respect us.

  Artemis, Lady,
  Huntress,
  We enter your presence,
  Respectfully,                                           130
  High pillars, roof gleaming gold,
  Respectfully we come,
  Women of Greece, we come,
  Green fields, soft rivers,
  Home.

  Lady, Iphigeneia, we're here.
  You sent for us, we're listening.
  Daughter of Agamemnon
  Who took a swarm of ships,
  A shoal, who toppled Troy –                             140
  Why did you call us, call us?

  *Enter* IPHIGENEIA.

IPHIGENEIA.
  Women,
  Weep for him,
  Wail for him,
  Aee aee,
  Weep for him,
  My brother, dead:
  Oh weep for him.
  I saw him, a dream in the dark, I saw him.             150
  He's gone. I'm nothing, dead.
  My father's palace, gone.
  Oee moee,

My loved ones, gone,
Feoo feoo, my Argos, pain.
God above, God plucked him,
My brother, plucked him,
Tumbled him to Hades.
160   Milk I'll pour for him, offerings:
Dark earth drinks milk,
Milk from upland herds,
Drinks yellow honey, wine,
Offerings, corpse-offerings.

Give me the bowl,
A gleam of gold for him,
Death-offerings, corpse-offerings.

Son of your father,
170   Son of Agamemnon,
For you these offerings.
Accept them.
No tomb you have,
Or I'd snip my hair,
Blonde hair, I'd weep for you.
I'm far away,
I've been torn away;
Your home, my home, all gone.
I was sacrificed, I'm dead.
The whole world knows. Oh weep.

CHORUS.
Weep with her, weep with her.
180   Beat breast, beat head, shriek, howl.
Death-songs, not living songs,
Sing with her.
Oee moee,
Weep for him,
Oee moee,
Gone from us,
Agamemnon's son,
Light of his father, hope.
How high they stood
In Argos,
How far they fell

In Argos,                                        190
Great ones,
Pain on pain.
Sun saw them,
Saw that evil, swerved;
Sun-horses blazing, blazing,
Turned aside from them.
A golden lamb,
Death, treachery, began it –
And now you die,
Princes of Argos, die:
Generation after generation                      200
God treads you down.

IPHIGENEIA.
God cursed me,
Laid traps for me,
There, in the dark,
In my mother's bed,
On the night I was conceived.
I was her daughter,
Klytemnestra's daughter,
I was the firstborn:                             210
I could have picked my prince,
Married any prince in Greece,
And they fattened me for sacrifice,
My father fattened me for sacrifice.
He sent a golden chariot to fetch me,
For Achilles they said,
To Aulis, to death, aee aee.
Now I sit out my life, alone,
With savages, in this wild place.
I've no husband, no child,
No city, no one.                                 220
Other women sit,
Sit with their women,
Weaving, singing,
Shuttles clacking, clacking,
Singing for Hera, Queen of Heaven,
Singing songs of Athene, warrior-queen.

Instead of this, shrieks are mine,
Blood, strangers' blood,
Altars wet with blood,
They shriek for mercy, shriek pain,
I weep for them. Orestes! Darling,
Dear little baby, at Mummy's breast,
230   In Mummy's arms, in Argos, Prince Orestes,
I weep for you, weep.

*Music ends.*

CHORUS.
Lady,
– Someone's coming,
– A herdsman.
– What is it?

*Enter* HERDSMAN.

HERDSMAN.
Lady, Your Reverence, I've news.

IPHIGENEIA.
240   What is it? Tell me calmly.

HERDSMAN.
Two men have come. In a boat,
Past the Clashing Rocks –
A sacrifice, for our Lady.
Get bowls, knives, corn. Be ready.

IPHIGENEIA.
Where are they from?

HERDSMAN.
By the look of them, Greece.

IPHIGENEIA.
Did you hear them speak? Use names?

HERDSMAN.
One of them called the other Pylades.

IPHIGENEIA.
250   You didn't hear the other name?

HERDSMAN.
No, Your Reverence.

IPHIGENEIA.
You saw them, caught them – how?

HERDSMAN.
We were on the shore, on the tide-line –

IPHIGENEIA.
Cattle-herders? Whatever for?

HERDSMAN.
Your Reverence, we wash them.

IPHIGENEIA.
Yes. Go on.
(*Aside.*) Greeks, here. It's time: on the altar,
The last Greek blood's long dry.
(*To the* HERDSMAN.) Tell me how you caught
    them.

HERDSMAN.
There's a channel, where the sea pounds in            260
Between the Clashing Rocks.
We'd brought our cattle there,
Down from the fields by the wood.
There's a cave there, with an overhang
Gouged out by the waves. Calm water.
Purple-fishers use it. That's where they were.
One of our men saw them,
Stepped back on tiptoe, whispered,
'Gods: look, gods.' Someone else –
Zealous – put his hands together, prayed:
'Palaimon, son of the sea-nymph, shiplord,            270
Smile on us. Kastor, Polydeukes, save us.
Children of Nereus,
Whose daughters were fifty sea-nymphs – '
Someone else interrupted him. Not so zealous.
'You're an idiot. They're shipwrecked sailors,
They know we sacrifice strangers,
They're scared. They're hiding.'
The rest of us agreed with him:
We decided to catch them,
As offerings for our Lady.                            280

One of them jumps up suddenly,

Starts jerking his head, rolling his eyes, shaking.
A maniac. 'Haraa! Haroo!
There she is. Pylades, there.
A dragon from Hell, snakes writhing,
She's after me. Fire, blood,
She's breathing fire, fanning it with her wings.
She's holding my mother, a rock,
290     A cliff, she'll throw it, she'll kill me, oee moee.'
Of course there was nothing there –
Dogs barking, cattle bellowing:
He thought they were the Furies.
We stayed where we were,
Didn't know what to do.
Next minute
He draws his sword, runs at the cattle –
Roaring, a lion – stabs, chops,
Fighting his Furies.
300     Sand salty with blood.
Well, we weren't having that –
Our cattle, our charges?
We picked up sticks, stones,
We shouted for help, blew our horns for help.
I mean, it was dangerous: we're cowherds,
No match for armed young warriors.

A crowd soon gathered. He'd stopped shaking,
Fallen on the ground, he was foaming at the mouth.
We ran in, took our chance,
Started banging them: sticks, stones.
310     The other one propped his friend up,
Wiped his lips, wrapped him in his cloak –
A prince's cloak, close-woven –
Tried to protect him.
The first one recovers,
Up he jumps,
Sees a tidal wave of enemies,
Starts groaning and moaning.
We kept up the stones.
Then, suddenly, he shouts,
320     'Pylades, at them! Swords!

One for all and all for – '
That stopped us. Back we drew:
I mean, swords, sharp swords
Swinging round our heads. We ran:
Back up the slope, along the beach.
But we kept up the stones –
They couldn't watch all ways.
While they were driving some of us off,
The rest of us . . .
Your Reverence, it was amazing, unbelievable:          330
We threw a thousand stones, ten thousand –
And not a single one struck home.
They're clean, unscarred, ready for our Lady.
We grabbed them in the end. It wasn't brave:
We just crowded round them,
Bashed the swords from their hands,
And they fell in a heap, exhausted.
We took them to His Majesty;
He sent them straight on here to be sacrificed.

Your Reverence, pray for more like these,
More Greeks like these
To sacrifice, to make Greece pay
For what they did to you at Aulis –

CHORUS.
It's amazing.
– Unbelievable.
They came all this way,                                340
Past the Clashing Rocks –
– Who are they?

IPHIGENEIA.
Enough. You, fetch them.
As for the holy rites: I'll see to them.

   *Exit* HERDSMAN.

Greeks! Flesh and blood!
I was sorry for them once,
Wept for them once, when Greeks landed here,
When they came to me. Not now. Not now.
Orestes is dead. I dreamed it: dead.

350   No pity now – whoever lands here, no pity.
It's simple, women, simple:
Our tears are for ourselves,
We've none to spare.
Zeus could have sent *her* here,
Parted the Clashing Rocks and sent *her* here,
Helen who ate my life, or him, Menelaos –
Sent them for me to kill, with my own hands,
For what they did, for Aulis.
They handled me like a calf,
Greeks handled me, for sacrifice.
360   My father took the knife;
I held out my hands;
I touched him: rough chin, my father.
'You said it was marriage, Daddy.
You lied to me. You're murdering me,
And listen! at home Mummy's singing,
Singing, flutes are playing,
People are dancing, they're happy,
They don't know you're murdering me.
Marriage! To Death, to the Underworld,
370   Swift chariot riding me here to blood, to die.'
Before, there in the palace, I stood there,
Head veiled, my eyes full of tears.
I was a child, embarrassed.
I wouldn't kiss my brother,
Wouldn't hug him goodbye,
Wouldn't kiss Elektra my sister.
I was embarrassed.
'It's only a marriage,' I thought.
'I'll see them again,
I'll visit them in Argos, I'll kiss them then.'

And now he's dead. Orestes is dead.
What a man you must have been,
What a son, your father's son . . .

380   Lady, Artemis, our Lady . . . How can I think
She insists on purity, clean hands, no blood,
Virgin servants – and takes human sacrifice?
Zeus' daughter! What gods eat human flesh?

My ancestor Tantalos, they say,
Served up his own son to feast the gods.
I'll not believe it. These people here,
These savages, they're cannibals,
They have a taste for flesh, and blame it on God.
God's foul? God's wicked? I won't think that. 390

Music.

CHORUS.

Dark rocks, dark sea, dark depths.
She came here once, from Argos,
The mad one, gadfly stung, flitting,
Skimming dark water, the mad one, Io.
These men, who are they?
What rivers nursed them
In Greece, in Greece –
Eurotas, perhaps,
Wide streams, green reeds, 400
Or Dirke, purest, holiest?
Here they come, here,
To this iron land, red altar,
Pillars red, temple red
With sailors' blood.
For gold? Was it for gold
They feathered our sea with oars,
Spread wings of sails,
Driving, driving,
Skimming dark water,
For gold, for gold? 410
It happens, often:
We hope, mortals hope,
Nothing kills it,
No mortal pain kills hope.
We scour the world,
Skim seas, visit strangers;
We hope, we think
We'll make our fortunes. 420
Some succeed, some don't;
All hope.

Rocks clash together –

How did they pass them?
Waves lurch and swell —
How did they pass them?
How did they come at last
To a quiet bay, calm water,
430   Sea-nymphs dancing, dancing,
Gulls, flocks of gulls,
White sand, soft breezes?
Why did they dare it, dare it?

Let her come,
Helen,
Sail to us,
Helen,
Sail here, land here,
Come to us,
440   Helen:
Let her stretch out her neck,
White throat,
Our mistress' hand,
Sharp knife.
Or better,
Let rescuers come,
Greeks, rescuers,
450   To take us home,
To answer our dreams,
Take us home to Greece.

Shh!
They're bringing them:
Two men, hands tied,
Flesh for our Lady.
— What the cowherd said was true:
460   They're bringing us Greeks,
Warriors, flesh for our Lady.

Lady, accept them. Blood-sacrifice,
If they please you, accept them.
It's the custom here:
Forget you're Greek, do it, do it.

*Music ends. Enter* ORESTES *and* PYLADES,
*guarded.*

IPHIGENEIA.
All right.
It must be properly done,
Well done. I'll see to it.
Untie their hands.
Do as I say:
They're offerings,
They mustn't be forced.
Go inside, get everything ready.                    470
You know what to do.

*Exeunt Guards.*

Feoo.
Your mother, who was she? Your father?
Your sister – did you have a sister?
How can she bear it, to lose such brothers?
It's Fate, God's will – who understands?
Pain on pain: it comes, it baffles us.
We pity you – to come so far,
And lie so long in death.                            480
We pity you.

ORESTES.
What's it to you?
Who are you?
You do this to us –
And weep? How dare you?
When a man's facing death, if he thinks
Someone else's sympathy will make it easier,
He's a fool. Double trouble:
Both a fool, and dead.
We knew what happens here, the sacrifices;
We took a chance; we lost.
You spare your tears.                                490

IPHIGENEIA.
One of you's Pylades. Which one?

ORESTES.
He is. Aren't you glad you asked?

IPHIGENEIA.
He's a Greek. Where from?

ORESTES.
Why d'you need to know?

IPHIGENEIA.
Are you his brother?

ORESTES.
In friendship, yes; not in blood.

IPHIGENEIA.
And your name?

ORESTES.
500   Unfortunate.

IPHIGENEIA.
Fate's to blame for that. And it's not what I asked.

ORESTES.
You don't need my name to kill me.

IPHIGENEIA.
It's too big a name to tell?

ORESTES.
You're killing a body, not a name.

IPHIGENEIA.
Where in Greece do you come from?

ORESTES.
What does it matter? I'm a corpse.

IPHIGENEIA.
And a surly one. Does it hurt to answer?

ORESTES.
I'm from Argos, glittering Argos.
You've heard of it?

IPHIGENEIA.
Where? In God's name. . . !

ORESTES.
510   Golden Mycenae, citadel of Argos.

IPHIGENEIA.
And you're an exile? You chose to leave?

ORESTES.
Yes. No.

IPHIGENEIA.
From Argos! At last, from Argos!

ORESTES.
Make the most of it. It's no use to me.

IPHIGENEIA.
Tell me something else. Please.

ORESTES.
No reason why I shouldn't, as things now are.

IPHIGENEIA.
Troy, in all the stories – you've heard of Troy?

ORESTES.
If only I hadn't.

IPHIGENEIA.
They say Troy's toppled. Gone.

ORESTES.
It's gone.                                                    520

IPHIGENEIA.
And Helen? Is she home with Menelaos?

ORESTES.
Oh, she's home. The death-bringer, oh, she's home.

IPHIGENEIA.
Where is she now? In Sparta?

ORESTES.
With her husband – the one she began with.

IPHIGENEIA.
Helen Hell-to-Men . . . I hate her.

ORESTES.
And I. I've come to hate her too.

IPHIGENEIA.
The Greeks are home from the war, all home?

ORESTES.
Have you got all night?

IPHIGENEIA.
Tell me what you know. Before you die.

ORESTES.
530   Ask one by one. I'll answer.

IPHIGENEIA.
Kalchas the prophet. Did he get home?

ORESTES.
Kalchas is dead. Or so they say.

IPHIGENEIA.
Dead! Thank you, Lady, thank you. Odysseus?

ORESTES.
He's alive, they say. Not home yet. Not dead.

IPHIGENEIA.
God keep him from home. God kill him.

ORESTES.
He's got troubles enough, they say.

IPHIGENEIA.
And Achilles, the sea-nymph's son. What of
    Achilles?

ORESTES.
He's dead. That marriage of his in Aulis: nothing.

IPHIGENEIA.
As I should know.

ORESTES.
540   You're well-informed on Greece. Who are you?

IPHIGENEIA.
Years ago, I was a child in Greece.

ORESTES.
Hence all these questions.

IPHIGENEIA.
What about that admiral?
The one they called Conqueror.

ORESTES.
Who d'you mean? What Conqueror?

IPHIGENEIA.
Son of Atreus. Agamemnon.

ORESTES.
Change the subject.

IPHIGENEIA.
What's the matter? Tell me!

ORESTES.
He's dead, alas –
And his death brought another death.

IPHIGENEIA.
Agamemnon dead. I weep for him.

ORESTES.
You knew him, did you?                               550

IPHIGENEIA.
That such a man should die.

ORESTES.
It was disgusting. His own wife butchered him.

IPHIGENEIA.
Blood for blood. He killed, he died. Alas.

ORESTES.
No more questions.

IPHIGENEIA.
Just one. His queen, Her Majesty . . . still alive?

ORESTES.
She's dead, by her own son's hand.

IPHIGENEIA.
O Argos. . . ! Why did he do it?

ORESTES.
Blood for blood. To avenge his father.

IPHIGENEIA.
Feoo. Well, of course, he was right.
But even so, to kill her . . .

ORESTES.
560   Right or wrong, God hunts him for it.

IPHIGENEIA.
His brothers, his sisters . . . are any left alive?

ORESTES.
One daughter: Elektra.

IPHIGENEIA.
Wasn't there another?
She was sacrificed, they said.

ORESTES.
Years ago. She's dead and gone.

IPHIGENEIA.
Poor child. Poor father, to kill his child.

ORESTES.
And all for that woman, that wife no-wife.

IPHIGENEIA.
The son, Agamemnon's son . . . he's still alive?

ORESTES.
For now – for what it's worth to him.

IPHIGENEIA.
He's alive! So much for dreams! Alive!

ORESTES.
570   Dreams, you say. I call the gods dreams.
Who can trust them? Our world's a mess –
And so is theirs. They send us dreams,
And prophets to explain them. Prophets!
Orestes listened to a prophet –
He was an intelligent man,
He listened to a prophet, and now he's . . .
You wouldn't believe what's become of him.

CHORUS.
Just a minute: us. What's to become of us?
And our parents, all our parents –
What's become of them?

IPHIGENEIA.
Listen. I've an idea. It could benefit us all,

Could be just what we need,
Could help us all. If I spare your life,                              580
Will you take them a message,
The people I know in Argos?
It's in a letter. I didn't write it myself,
I was too young to learn to write
When what happened . . . happened.
A prisoner wrote it, years ago:
He saw that I was trapped here,
That what I was doing was forced on me,
By our Lady's law, that I had no choice.
All I've needed since was someone
Who'd carry it to Argos, to people I know,
Someone I know, if I spared his life.                                 590

You come from Argos;
You know . . . the ones I know.
Save yourself. Take my letter.
It's easy, easy. *He* can die.
They'll be satisfied. They want a victim,
An offering for our Lady. He'll be enough.

ORESTES.
Just a minute. This all makes sense,
Except for one thing. I won't do it.
I'm the captain, this is my adventure,
He's the crewman. I can't skip free                                  600
Of trouble and leave my friend to die.
No, it's easy: give *him* the letter.
Let *him* take it to Argos, deliver it.
As for myself, I'm ready, for Death, whatever.
To buy one's own skin,
And condemn one's friends: no one does that.
If it's his life or mine, there's no more to say.

IPHIGENEIA.
So generous! So kind!
Such a worthy friend! A prince.                                      610
If only my brother could be like you.
That's right: I've a brother. I've never seen him,
He was a baby in arms when . . .
The letter: *he* can take the letter,

While you stay here and die. Your choice.

ORESTES.
Who kills? Who orders the sacrifice?

IPHIGENEIA.
I do. I'm Her Reverence: I do.

ORESTES.
Grim work, my lady: I pity you.

IPHIGENEIA.
620   Do you think I choose it? I do as I'm told.

ORESTES.
You lift the knife yourself?

IPHIGENEIA.
I sprinkle holy water. Pray.

ORESTES.
Who does the actual killing?
If you don't mind me asking.

IPHIGENEIA.
Temple servants, trained servants.

ORESTES.
And when the victims are dead, what burial?

IPHIGENEIA.
We burn them to ash on the altar fire,
Then bury them, in a hole in the temple floor . . .

ORESTES.
Feoo.
If only she were here, my sister –

IPHIGENEIA.
You're wasting your time.
Whoever you are, your sister isn't here.
630   This is the ends of the earth, not Greece.
But since you're from Argos, my Argos,
I'll play her part, I'll see to it:
Flowers in the fire, green olive-oil, honey,
Wild mountain-flowers distilled –
And a monument, a fine memorial.
The letter, I'll fetch the letter,

I'll do everything I can. It's not my fault.
Guards, leave them unbound, but watch them.
(*Aside to herself, as she goes*.) They'll get the letter, in
   Argos.
They'll know I'm alive, against all hope.
My darling, he'll know, he'll know.

> *Exit. Music.* [*Note: in the original,* ORESTES' *and*
> PYLADES' *lines were spoken interjections in a*
> *choral song.*]

CHORUS.
We weep for you, weep.
Blood, death, sacrifice.

ORESTES.
There's no need for tears, but thanks.

CHORUS.
We smile for you, smile.
Safe, home, return.

PYLADES.
I leave my friend to die.                                  650

CHORUS.
A path of tears.
– Feoo, feoo. One dies.
– Aee aee. But which?
Which one must we weep for, which?
– One dies, one lives;
Whose fate is more fearful, whose?

> *Music ends.*

ORESTES.
Pylades, are you thinking what I'm thinking?

PYLADES.
How can I say unless you tell me?

ORESTES.
I mean, that woman. Who is she?                            660
Greek, she spoke Greek. All those questions:
What happened at Troy,
How the generals got home,

That prophet Kalchas, Achilles,
Unfortunate Agamemnon – did you see her start
When his name came up? – his wife, his children.
She has to be Greek, from Argos,
Else why the letter,
Why else go on about Argos
As if her life depended on it?

PYLADES.
That's right: the two kings, everyone knows
670   What happened to them. But never mind that.
There's something else, far more important.

ORESTES.
What? Tell me.

PYLADES.
I'm to live and you're to die.
I sailed with you, I should die with you.
I'm not going to Argos, to Phokis,
To be called a traitor, a coward.
You know what people are like. They'll say
I saved my own skin by betraying you,
680   Or perhaps I killed you, took advantage of your . . .
Problems to snatch your throne.
I'm Elektra's husband, remember?
Your heir apparent. I can't have that;
I won't have that. I'm your friend:
If they're going to butcher you and burn you
They can do the same to me.
It's what friendship's for.

ORESTES.
Don't be ridiculous. I've enough to bear,
Don't give me this as well.
Suppose I survive and you get killed –
690   Won't people think the same of me,
That I betrayed my own best friend?
God hates me; I'm happy to die;
What's life to me? You're rich,
You've a palace, a country,
You're not involved in this.

Go home to Elektra, have children —
Why else d'you think I gave her to you?
They'll keep our name alive, our royal name,
Our father's name. Live! Go on, live!
Be king! Enjoy it! Just one thing:
When you come to Greece,                              700
To Argos where horses breed, do this for me:
Build a tomb, a memorial,
Let Elektra weep for me, chop her hair for me,
A lock of hair, offered for Orestes.
Tell her how I died, cut down, by a woman,
By one of our own, an Argive.
And never desert her: you're all she'll have.
We'll be gone, her family, gone.
Goodbye, old friend, dear old friend:
We hunted together, were boys together,
You shared my every burden.                          710

Apollo lied to me.
I did as he said before, he took advantage,
He sent me here, to the ends of the earth,
Far from Greece, my Greece. I gave him my life,
I murdered my mother — he ordered it —
And I destroyed myself.

PYLADES.
    Dear friend, I'll build a memorial,
    I'll love Elektra. You'll be
    As dear to me in death as you were in life.
    Unless . . . Is the oracle over yet?
    Fulfilled? There could be more.                  720
    Granted, they're just about to kill you,
    But one never knows. Amazing things happen:
    You just can't tell.

ORESTES.
    Oh yes you can.
    She's coming. It's too late now.

        *Enter* IPHIGENEIA.

IPHIGENEIA.
    Guards, inside.

They're getting everything ready: help them.

*Exeunt Guards.*

Here's the letter: pages and pages.
Now listen, carefully. I mean,
A man's not the same when he's safe and well
730   As when he's staring death in the face.
Whichever of you leaves for Argos,
I don't want him tearing up this letter
As soon as he's safely out of harbour.
It has to be delivered.

ORESTES.
What d'you suggest?

IPHIGENEIA.
An oath. He swears
To take it to Argos, to the people named.

ORESTES.
And you swear as well?

IPHIGENEIA.
Swear to do what?

ORESTES.
To grant him safe passage out of here.

IPHIGENEIA.
740   Well, naturally. How else could he take my letter?

ORESTES.
What about His Majesty?

IPHIGENEIA.
I'll persuade His Majesty.
I'll take your friend on board in person.

ORESTES.
Pylades, swear. Your Reverence: the words.

IPHIGENEIA.
'I promise to deliver this letter faithfully – '

PYLADES.
I promise.

IPHIGENEIA.
And I promise
To take you beyond the Clashing Rocks.

PYLADES.
In whose name d'you promise?

IPHIGENEIA.
Our Lady, Artemis.

PYLADES.
And I swear in Zeus' name, Omnipotent.

IPHIGENEIA.
If you break your oath? 750

PYLADES.
May I drown. And you?

IPHIGENEIA.
May I never see Greece again.

PYLADES.
Hang on. There is one thing.

IPHIGENEIA.
Say it. If it's reasonable, let's hear it.

PYLADES.
Suppose my ship sinks, and the letter's gone,
And I've nothing left except what I stand up in?
What happens then?

IPHIGENEIA.
It's easy.
I'll tell you what's in the letter; 760
Then, if it's lost, you can tell
My friends in person. So it's doubly sure:
Either the letter gives my friends its message,
Or if it's lost, and you survive, you tell them.

PYLADES.
That's reasonable. Start with their names,
Then the message. Who's the letter for?

IPHIGENEIA.
Orestes, Prince Orestes of Argos,
Agamemnon's son. Tell him,

Iphigeneia's still alive. His sister.
770    The whole world thought she died at Aulis,
But she didn't.

ORESTES.
She's still alive? Where is she?

IPHIGENEIA.
I'm here. Don't interrupt.
Tell him to come and fetch me home.
I'm a servant of Artemis,
In a country of savages,
Forced to murder strangers –

ORESTES.
Pylades, help me. What's going on?

IPHIGENEIA.
Say, if he doesn't, I'll haunt him forever.

PYLADES.
Orestes . . .

IPHIGENEIA.
That's the name. Orestes. Remember it.

ORESTES.
780    O gods . . .

IPHIGENEIA.
Now what's the matter?

ORESTES.
Nothing. I was thinking . . .
(*Aside to himself.*) Ask no questions. Wait and see.

IPHIGENEIA.
Tell him Artemis, our Lady, saved me.
When my father lifted the knife,
She put a deer in my place
And brought me here.
That's what you say;
That's what the letter says.

PYLADES.
Your Reverence, it's easy.
I swore an oath, I'll do it,

I'll do it now. It's easy, look.                           790
Orestes, your sister sent this letter,
I deliver it, it's yours.

ORESTES.
Thanks.
But what do I need with paper?
Keep it!
Sister. Darling.
I can't believe it.
I'm dreaming.
It isn't happening. Hold me.

CHORUS.
Stop! How dare you?
Touch Her Reverence!
Sacrilege! How dare you?

ORESTES.
Sister. Agamemnon's child.
My sister. Don't push me away,                             800
Your brother. I'm here.

IPHIGENEIA.
You're joking. My brother's in Argos.

ORESTES.
He's not. I'm not. I'm here.

IPHIGENEIA.
Klytemnestra's son.

ORESTES.
And Agamemnon's.

IPHIGENEIA.
How can you prove it?

ORESTES.
Family secrets.

IPHIGENEIA.
What are they? Tell me!                                    810

ORESTES.
Elektra said . . . There was a quarrel . . .
Our grandfather and grand-uncle . . .

Atreus, Thyestes, they quarrelled –

IPHIGENEIA.
About the golden lamb.

ORESTES.
That's right. She said you made a picture.
You were just a little girl . . .

IPHIGENEIA.
Darling – every word you say –

ORESTES.
The sun turned backwards –

IPHIGENEIA.
I put that in the picture too.

ORESTES.
Your mother sent wedding-offerings to Aulis –

IPHIGENEIA.
And then there was no wedding –

ORESTES.
820   You sent Klytemnestra funeral-offerings –

IPHIGENEIA.
Instead of a body, a lock of hair.

ORESTES.
Just one more proof. I saw
On your bedroom wall at home:
Pelops' spear, the one he took,
Great-great-grandfather,
When he went to kill Oinomaos, win a wife –

IPHIGENEIA.
Orestes. It's you.
Dear brother. Darling.
830   Mine. Here from Argos,
In this iron land. Mine.

ORESTES.
Iphigeneia.
Dead, you were dead:
They told me.
You're alive.

Tears.
Your cheeks are wet.
Mine, wet.
Tears, tears of happiness.

IPHIGENEIA.
You were just a baby,
In your nurse's arms.
I left you,
And now you're here.
Happiness. I can't find words.                                840

ORESTES.
We'll be together,
Forever now,
Happy now, forever.

IPHIGENEIA.
Women, friends: a dream.
Happiness: I hold it,
It's in my hands,
I'm holding it. Don't let it fly.
Argos, Mycenae, you bore him, Orestes,
My brother, our light, our hope.

ORESTES.
Dear sister.                                                850
Nobility is ours, a noble house.
But what blesses us, curses us:
Pain on pain.

IPHIGENEIA.
Father held a knife.
It touched my throat.

ORESTES.
I dream it. Oee moee.
I don't see it, I dream it.

IPHIGENEIA.
They made me a bride, sang hymns –
But not for Achilles. I was to marry Death.
Sky wept with singing, wept for me.                          860
Feoo feoo. Not marriage, murder.

ORESTES.
Father did it. How could he?

IPHIGENEIA.
Father no-father,
Crime, pain, death,
Fate drags us, drags us.

ORESTES.
You'd have killed your brother.

IPHIGENEIA.
Don't say it. Darling.
It's horrible.
I'd have – horrible.
870    Fate saved you,
Snatched you from these hands, these hands.
What happens now?
What else can Fate do?
How can I save you,
Send you home
From this altar,
This iron land,
To Argos, our Argos,
880    Not spill your blood?
Think.
Iphigeneia, find a way.
Leave your ship,
Run away.
No: savages,
Trackless forests,
Certain death.
Sail, then,
890    Sail past Clashing Rocks,
Find a way, escape.
Iphigeneia, how?
Who'll help?
What god? What mortal?
A miracle, light gleaming, gleaming,
For the children of Argos, hope.

*Music ends.*

CHORUS.
   It's happening.
   – It's not a story.                                      900
   – We're seeing it ourselves.
   – It's real.

PYLADES.
   Orestes, it's not surprising:
   Your long-lost sister,
   Hugging, kissing, it's understandable.
   But it's time to think about escaping,
   Out of here, with honour.
   Fate's ours: we must take it.
   This is no time for tears.

ORESTES.
   You're right. God's with us,
   And the more we help ourselves,                          910
   The more he'll help us.

IPHIGENEIA.
   Just one thing. There's time. Elektra,
   My sister, my darling – is Elektra still alive?

ORESTES.
   She's alive and happy. This is her husband.

IPHIGENEIA.
   Pylades.

ORESTES.
   Prince of Phokis. Strophios' son.

IPHIGENEIA.
   Agamemnon's nephew. Our cousin.

ORESTES.
   My one true friend.

IPHIGENEIA.
   He wasn't even born when Father, in Aulis –              920

ORESTES.
   Strophios had children later.

IPHIGENEIA.
   Pylades, cousin –

ORESTES.
More than cousin. He saved my life –

IPHIGENEIA.
When you killed our mother.
How could you bear it – ?

ORESTES.
I avenged our father. Leave it.

IPHIGENEIA.
She killed our father –
Killed her own husband. Why?

ORESTES.
I said, leave it. You don't want to hear.

IPHIGENEIA.
If you say so. You're king in Argos now?

ORESTES.
Menelaos rules. I'm exiled.

IPHIGENEIA.
930   Uncle Menelaos took advantage, banished you?

ORESTES.
I was afraid of the Furies. I ran from them.

IPHIGENEIA.
So that's why you – on the beach just now –

ORESTES.
It happens. People see it.

IPHIGENEIA.
The Furies, our mother's Furies.

ORESTES.
They whip. Blood-whips. My blood.

IPHIGENEIA.
But why come here?

ORESTES.
Apollo sent me. His oracle sent me.

IPHIGENEIA.
Why? God's oracle: can you tell it?

ORESTES.
> I can tell it, tell all my misery. After I . . .
> After what happened to Klytemnestra,     940
> The Furies chased me, hunting-dogs,
> An exile, all the way to Athens.
> Apollo sent me there, for trial.
> My accusers: the Nameless Ones.
> They've a court there,
> Established by Zeus himself
> Years ago, the Areiopagos . . .
> I was cursed by God, a murderer.
> No one welcomed me or gave me shelter.
> They fed me, alone,
> At a table in the courtyard,
> Away from the family,     950
> Gave me separate food, wine,
> Forbade me to speak.
> I could share, but not join in.
> I put up with it, I smiled, said nothing –
> But inside, I was weeping,
> Screaming, 'I killed my mother!'
> (Ever since, I'm told,
> They've commemorated my arrival in the city,
> Commemorated what happened,
> With a feast for Athene: the Feast of Jugs.)     960
> It came to the trial. On Areiopagos Hill,
> I stood on one side, the defendant,
> Their leader, the Furies' leader on the other,
> The accuser. They charged me: matricide.
> I defended myself. Apollo spoke up for me.
> They counted the votes. Equal.
> Athene gave her casting vote – for mercy.
> I was acquitted, not guilty of murder.
> Some of the Furies accepted, took up residence
> In a cave not far from the court. The rest
> Pelted after me again, hunting-dogs,     970
> Till I came again to Delphi, to Apollo's temple.
> I was starving, on my knees.
> I begged him, 'You destroyed me,
> Save me, or let me kill myself.'

A voice from the inner shrine,
The golden throne – Apollo's voice.
He sent me here. There's a statue,
Artemis' statue, it fell from the sky,
I've to take it to Athens,
980    Set it up in Athens, and they'll leave me,
My madness will leave me,
We'll escape, you and I, sail home to Argos,
Rule again in Argos. Sister, darling, help me –
For Argos, our royal house, for all of us.
Unless we have that statue, life ends for us.

CHORUS.
Generation after generation,
God curses the great ones of Argos,
God stamps them down.

IPHIGENEIA.
Home to Argos.
I prayed for that,
Darling brother,
990    To sail home, see you –
And then you came.
We can end our agony, you say,
Restore our royal house,
I can forgive my father
Who raised his knife to me,
I can go home. I want it,
I won't shed your blood, I want it.
But I'm afraid of Artemis, our Lady,
Of His Majesty, when he finds
The shrine empty, the statue gone.
I'll die. They won't listen to me, I'll die.
Take me with you.
Take the statue, take me,
1000    Take both of us. Risk it.
If you can't, take the statue, leave me:
I'll die but you'll be safe, I'll have saved you.
You're a man, your family's future;
I'm a woman, nothing.

ORESTES.
  I took our mother's blood;
  I'll not take yours.
  In all that happens,
  Life or death, we're equal:
  We escape together, go home together,                    1010
  Or die together. And another thing:
  If stealing this statue was to offend our Lady,
  Why did Apollo send me here to do it?
  He can't have cheated me – he brought me you!
  It's obvious: he wants us home.

IPHIGENEIA.
  But how can we do it?
  Steal the statue,
  Save our lives, get home –
  How can we do it?

ORESTES.
  If we killed His Majesty. . . ?                           1020

IPHIGENEIA.
  I won't. I owe him my life.

ORESTES.
  If you want to escape, you owe him his death.

IPHIGENEIA.
  I can't. I'm sorry.

ORESTES.
  Suppose you hid me inside the temple?

IPHIGENEIA.
  Till it's dark, you mean – then run for it?

ORESTES.
  Bright day's for honest folk; night favours thieves.

IPHIGENEIA.
  There are temple guards. They'd find us.

ORESTES.
  We're finished, then. What else can we do?

IPHIGENEIA.
  Perhaps . . . I might . . . it might work . . .

ORESTES.
1030    What? Tell me!

IPHIGENEIA.
What's happened to you . . . I could use it.

ORESTES.
How? Tell me: a woman's plan.

IPHIGENEIA.
I'll tell His Majesty
You're unclean, a matricide.

ORESTES.
What good will that do?

IPHIGENEIA.
You can't be sacrificed.

ORESTES.
Of course.

IPHIGENEIA.
Victims must be clean.

ORESTES.
But how does that help with the statue?

IPHIGENEIA.
I'll take you to the shore to purify you.

ORESTES.
1040    And leave the statue here?

IPHIGENEIA.
No. You touched it;
It needs to be purified as well –

ORESTES.
In sea-water, there on the shore –

IPHIGENEIA.
Where your ship lies waiting.

ORESTES.
Will you carry it yourself, the statue?

IPHIGENEIA.
No one else can touch it.

ORESTES.
  And Pylades?

IPHIGENEIA.
  He shares your blood-guilt: I'll tell them that.

ORESTES.
  Tell His Majesty?

IPHIGENEIA.
  I'll persuade him.

ORESTES.
  My crew'll be waiting.                                    1050

IPHIGENEIA.
  You see to that.

ORESTES.
  One thing only: these women,
  They mustn't blab. Persuade them,
  Ask them nicely, play for sympathy,
  As women do. I'll see to all the rest.

        *Exeunt* ORESTES *and* PÝLADES.

IPHIGENEIA.
  Women, dearest friends, I look to you.
  I'm in your hands: to go on living,
  Or to be blotted out, no sister beloved,
  No brother, no native land.
  What can I say? We're women,                              1060
  Women help each other,
  Protect each other, keep confidence.
  Help us escape. Don't inform on us. Support us.
  Three people, three fates, lie in your hands:
  Shall we sail safely home, or die?

        *She goes to them individually.*

  I'll come back,
  You know I'll come back,
  I'll fetch you home to Greece.
  Hold my hand. Kiss me. Your cheek.
  Think of them waiting for news:
  Your mother, your father, your children . . .             1070

(*To them all:*) You'll do it? Say you'll do it.
Yes, or no.
My poor brother, myself –
Please save our lives.

CHORUS.
Lady, my dear, you're safe.
Get safe away.
– In Zeus' name I swear:
I'll keep silence.
– No word from me.
– Your secret, what you ask: you're safe.

IPHIGENEIA.
God bless you. God reward you.
1080   He'll be on his way, His Majesty,
Coming to check on the sacrifice.

Artemis, Lady,
You saved my life before, at Aulis:
Save us now, all three of us,
Or prove Apollo false.
Come with us,
Leave these savages, this iron land,
Come to Athens;
They'll smile to welcome you.

  *Exit. Music.*

CHORUS.
Seagulls, mewing,
1090   Sharp cliffs, harsh cries,
Lovers' cries, lost love –
We weep with you,
Weep with you.
Flightless, lost here,
For Greece we cry:
For our Lady in Greece we cry,
Palm-fringes, laurel,
1100   Grey-green olive,
Water of rippling lake,
Swans singing, singing.

Teardrops falling,

Soft cheeks, sharp tears,
Soldiers came,
Men came,                                         1110
Stole us for this, for this:
Slavery, slaves,
For our Lady,
Red altars steaming with blood,
Human blood, lost ones,
Weep for them, weep,
No choice is theirs, they die,                    1120
Happy once, no more.

Princess, sail now,
Sail for Argos,
Oars beat, flutes squeal,
Pan-pipes for you,
Apollo plays for you,                             1130
Scudding, scudding,
For Athens, Athens,
Dark water, foam,
Wind bellies your sails
And you desert us.

If I'd wings, had wings,
See me soaring,
Fluttering, roosting,                             1140
There where I was born.
Home, tired, resting.
Hear them,
Dancing,
Weddings,
Dancing,
I dance with them,
Bright headdress flying,
Hair streaming, streaming.

> *Music ends. Enter* THOAS, *attended.*

THOAS.
That Greek woman, where is she,
The one in charge? Has she finished yet?
Is the fire lit, are bodies burning? Well?

CHORUS.
> She's coming, lord. She'll tell it all.

> *Enter* IPHIGENEIA, *carrying the statue.*

THOAS.
> The statue. Where are you going?

IPHIGENEIA.
> Be still, lord. Still.

THOAS.
1160   Inside, something's happened.

IPHIGENEIA.
> Back! In our Lady's name.

THOAS.
> What's happened? Tell me.

IPHIGENEIA.
> They're unclean. Your prisoners, lord.

THOAS.
> Who told you?

IPHIGENEIA.
> The statue moved.

THOAS.
> Was there an earthquake?

IPHIGENEIA.
> It moved by itself. It moved. It shut its eyes.

THOAS.
> Because of these Greeks? Unclean?

IPHIGENEIA.
> They're murderers.

THOAS.
1170   Who's murdered? My men, on shore?

IPHIGENEIA.
> In Greece. They came here unclean.

THOAS.
> Who died? Speak!

IPHIGENEIA.
The mother. They hacked her, both.

THOAS.
Apollo! They call us savages!

IPHIGENEIA.
They've been hounded out of Greece.

THOAS.
That's why you're bringing the statue —

IPHIGENEIA.
Outside, into clean, fresh air.

THOAS.
How did you know they were murderers?

IPHIGENEIA.
When the statue moved, I asked them why.

THOAS.
Only a Greek would think of that.

IPHIGENEIA.
They tried to charm me.                                    1180

THOAS.
Sweet talk from Argos?

IPHIGENEIA.
Orestes, my only brother, 's well.

THOAS.
They bring good news, you spare their lives.

IPHIGENEIA.
So they hoped. My father's well. All's well.

THOAS.
But you didn't listen. You serve our Lady.

IPHIGENEIA.
I hate all Greeks. Greece ended me.

THOAS.
What shall we do with them?

IPHIGENEIA.
The law's laid down. We must obey it —

THOAS.
1190   With offering-pots and knives. Go, now.

IPHIGENEIA.
First, I must purify them.

THOAS.
How? Fresh water? Salt?

IPHIGENEIA.
In the sea. It cleans all mortal filth.

THOAS.
So they'll be clean, for our Lady.

IPHIGENEIA.
And so will I, I pray.

THOAS.
Do it here, in the bay beside the temple.

IPHIGENEIA.
In a secret place. The rites are secret.

THOAS.
Wherever you like. I won't interfere.

IPHIGENEIA.
I must purify the statue too.

THOAS.
1200   They polluted it – the mother's blood.

IPHIGENEIA.
That's why I took it from its plinth.

THOAS.
Say what must be done.

IPHIGENEIA.
First, tie their hands.

THOAS.
You think they'll escape? Where to?

IPHIGENEIA.
They're Greeks.

THOAS.
Guards, see to it.

IPHIGENEIA.
  Then bring them out here.

THOAS (*to the Guards*).
  Do it.

IPHIGENEIA.
  Cover their heads.

THOAS.
  They mustn't pollute the sun.

IPHIGENEIA.
  Send attendants with me.

THOAS.
  You men: go with her.

IPHIGENEIA.
  Send orders to the people.

THOAS.
  What orders?

IPHIGENEIA.
  To stay indoors.

THOAS.
  To avoid pollution.                                    1210

IPHIGENEIA.
  Exactly.

THOAS.
  You, fellow: tell them.

IPHIGENEIA.
  No one must see them.

THOAS.
  You protect my people.

IPHIGENEIA.
  And others, nearer . . .

THOAS.
  You mean me.

  IPHIGENEIA *indicates 'Yes'*.

All hear and obey. What must I do?

IPHIGENEIA.
>    Stay here in the temple.
>    Purify it. Burn incense, pray.

THOAS.
>    I'll see to it.

IPHIGENEIA.
>    When the Greeks come out,
>    Lift your cloak, veil your eyes.

THOAS.
>    To avoid pollution.

IPHIGENEIA.
>    If I take some time, don't be alarmed.

THOAS.
1220    Holy work. Take what time you need.

IPHIGENEIA.
>    Holy work. God help us.

THOAS.
>    God help us.

>    *Guards bring* ORESTES *and* PYLADES *from the temple.*

IPHIGENEIA.
>    The Greeks are coming.
>    Fresh clothes for our Lady;
>    Lambs for sacrifice; lamps –
>    All I ordered for the ceremony.

>    *A procession forms.*

>    Beware! People of this land, beware pollution.
>    Temple servants, brides, pregnant women,
>    Beware! Go in, avoid pollution.
1230    Lady, hear us. We wash away their guilt,
>    Make holy sacrifice, purify your holy place.
>    Help us, bless us. Lady, our secret prayers,
>    Hear them. God grant all these our prayers.

>    *Exeunt all but* CHORUS. *Music.*

CHORUS.
   In an orchard long ago
   On Delos, on Delos,
   Our Lady Leto bore children,
   A son, a daughter, twins:
   Golden-haired Apollo, who plays the lute,
   Our Lady Artemis, who hunts with the bow.
   She brought them then, their mother,
   From rocky isle to Delphi, Parnassos' peaks       1240
   Where Dionysos dances,
   Where springs of pure water flow,
   Where a dragon,
   Rainbow scales, blood eyes, bronze body,
   No monster its equal on sea or land,
   Sat watching, coiled watching,
   On the navel of the earth, on guard.
   Apollo killed it there,                      1250
   A baby wriggling in his mother's arms,
   Killed it,
   Sat on the golden throne,
   Our prophet, prophet of the world,
   By the holy spring
   At the navel of the earth.

   At the navel of the earth,
   In Delphi, in Delphi,                      1260
   Mother Earth saw her dragon killed,
   Spilled dreams from dark womb,
   Dream-shapes flitting, billowing,
   Dark billowing in mortal minds,
   Dream-shapes, in darkness, dark,
   Whispering, whispering the future.
   Apollo's privilege, stolen.
   Up he sprang, to Olympos,                1270
   Baby fingers touched Zeus' throne,
   Baby voice demanded rescue,
   Help for Delphi,
   Rescue from Mother Earth,
   Her rage, her plots, her plans.
   'Don't let her steal it, Father —

My honour, mortals honour me,
Don't let her steal it.'
Zeus laughed. 'It's granted,
What you ask, it's granted.
1280   The future now
Is yours to tell, yours only, now.'

*Music ends. Enter* ATTENDANT.

ATTENDANT.
Guards! Priests! His Majesty,
Where's His Majesty? Open the doors,
Call His Majesty. Call him.

CHORUS.
What's the matter?
– If a woman may speak unbidden.

ATTENDANT.
They're gone. The Greeks are gone.
1290   She did it. Iphigeneia's gone.
Our Lady's statue is gone,
Dumped in the hold like cargo.

CHORUS.
His Majesty's not here.
– He hurried away.
– Just now, he went just now.

ATTENDANT.
I must find him, tell him.

CHORUS.
Run after him. You'll find him.
Then you can tell him.

ATTENDANT.
I don't believe you. Women!
You're part of this.

CHORUS.
1300   Ridiculous! Us – help Greeks escape?
Go to the palace. Run.

ATTENDANT.
In a minute. First: hey, inside, open up!

Is His Majesty there? Is anyone there?
Tell him: disaster. It's happened. Now.

*Enter* THOAS.

THOAS.
Shouting, banging. This is our Lady's temple.
What's the matter?

ATTENDANT.
Feoo.
They said you'd gone, they told me . . .                    1310
And you were inside all the time, not gone.

THOAS.
Why did they lie?

ATTENDANT.
Later, Majesty. Listen:
Her Reverence has gone, Iphigeneia,
Gone with those Greeks, with the statue, gone.
'I'll purify it,' she said. She tricked us.

THOAS.
What possessed her?

ATTENDANT.
She did it to save Orestes.

THOAS.
Orestes of Argos?

ATTENDANT.
Our Greek, our victim, was Orestes.                          1320

THOAS.
God's work was here.

ATTENDANT.
Lord, listen. We have to catch them.
Think it out: we must catch them. How?

THOAS.
Tell me how it happened.
We'll catch them:
They can sail as far as they like,
They won't outsail my spears.

ATTENDANT.
We went to the shore: Her Reverence,
1330    The Greeks, us servants, exactly as you ordered.
Orestes' ship was there, at anchor, hidden.
'Stay here,' Her Reverence told us.
'No one must see the ritual. It's forbidden.'
We stayed, they went: the Greeks, hands tied,
Her Reverence behind them, holding the rope.
We didn't like it, lord, but we had our orders.

We couldn't see them. But we heard:
Shrieks, wild shrieks, outlandish shrieks,
As if she was doing some magic.
Silence. We began to get itchy:
1340    Had they killed her, perhaps, broken free,
Murdered her and run for it? We sat there:
The ritual was secret, we'd orders.
But in the end, we all decided:
Orders, no orders, we had to go.

That's when we found the ship.
A warship, Greek, two lines of oars
Lifted high like wings, fifty rowers, poised.
Our prisoners were on the shore, untied,
Men were steadying the ship for them,
1350    Others letting down ladders, rope-ladders,
To haul them in.
When we saw what they were doing,
Saw the trick, we ran,
Grabbed Her Reverence,
Grabbed the anchor-ropes,
Tried to pull away the steering-oars.
'Bastards! Who are you,
Stealing our statue, our priestess?
1360    Who the hell d'you think you are?'
'Orestes,' that's what he answered.
'I'm Orestes: her brother,
Her long-lost brother,
And I'm taking her home.'

We were holding her.
We tried to drag her away –

We paid for that: black eyes.
Neither side was armed: not us, not them.
But they pummelled us,
Feet, fists, whirlwinds of fists:
They put their marks on us.                          1370
We dropped back,
Heads, faces bleeding,
Up the beach, where it was safer.
We started throwing stones.
Some sailors with bows and arrows
Appeared on deck, started shooting.
We moved out of range.
A sudden wave washed in,
The ship shifted. Iphigeneia
Didn't want to get her feet wet.                     1380
Her brother picked her up, grabbed the ladder,
Thigh-deep in the water, scrambled on board.
So there they were: our priestess,
Our Lady's statue, safe on board.

Someone was shouting,
'Row, Greeks, row for your lives!
We risked the Clashing Rocks for this,
We've got it. Row!'
They all started shouting, cheering.                 1390
Oars foamed in sea.
The ship moved, glided.
In the bay, still water;
In the open sea, big waves.
They were driven back to land;
They bent their oars, fought the current,
But it was no good. The ship leapt for the rocks.
Then up she stood, Her Reverence,
Began praying. 'Our Lady,
Lady Artemis, save us: your priestess,
My rescuers. Save us, carry us safe
From this savage land to Greece.
You love your brother, Lady: Artemis, Apollo.
I love my brother. Save us. Save us.'                1400

The sailors started singing,

Singing to Apollo.
Their oars were like wings,
Beating, beating.
But the undertow was stronger:
The ship edged nearer,
Loomed on the rocks.
A man jumped overboard,
They threw him a rope,
He tried to moor it safe.
Your Majesty, now!
1410    Hurry, now! I ran to tell you.
Bring ropes, chains, now.
Unless the tide changes, they're done for.
Poseidon, Lord Poseidon, enemy of Greece,
Enemy of Argos, has put them in our hands.
Orestes is yours, is ours,
And that woman, that sister,
Who was snatched from death at Aulis
And pays God back with this, with this!

CHORUS.
1420    Iphigeneia, poor lady;
Orestes, trapped.
You're in their hands,
You've failed. You're caught.

THOAS.
Horses! To horse! Pelt there, snatch them,
Wait till they ground, then snatch them.
Hunt them, for her, for our Lady,
They snapped their fingers at our Lady,
Hunt them, stop them. Ships, launch ships.
Land, sea, ride them down, snatch them,
1430    Toss them, spike them. You, women:
You knew of this, you're dead.
As soon as I've time,
As soon as it's done, you're dead.

*Enter* ATHENE.

ATHENE.
Stop. Majesty, how far will you go with this?

Athene speaks. Call off this rush of men.
Apollo ordered this. By his command
Orestes fled from the Furies, here,
To rescue his sister, carry the holy statue                    1440
To Athens, my city, to be free at last.
Hear me. Poseidon won't drown Orestes
As you believe.
Already he's calmed the sea,
He's given them fair sailing.
I asked it, he did it.

Orestes, hear me.
Far out to sea, but hear me.
Take the statue, take your sister. You're safe.
And when you come to Athens, built by gods,
There's a sacred place, on the edge of the plain.           1450
Build a temple there, our Lady's shrine,
Her statue. They'll come there,
They'll worship our Lady there,
They'll remember your torment,
Your Furies, your voyage to this savage place,
Your triumph. Tell them:
When they sacrifice, on holy days,
Their priests must choose a man,
Draw a knife, nick his throat
And draw one drop of blood,                                       1460
In our Lady's name, in Artemis' name:
Your ransom.

Iphigeneia, serve her there:
Guard her shrine, keep the sacred keys.
And on the day you die
They'll bury you there, they'll wrap you in silk,
Silk gowns, offerings to our Lady
From women who died in childbirth.
Thoas, send these women home to Greece.
I order it. Be satisfied.
Orestes, when you were tried in Athens,
And the votes were equal, I saved you.                          1470
I voted for mercy, I spared your life.
Let this be a precedent forever:

Where votes are equal, the accused
Must be acquitted, not condemned.
Son of Agamemnon, take your sister home.
Thoas, be satisfied.

THOAS.
Athene, Lady, only fools
Hear orders from the gods
And disobey. I'm satisfied.
Orestes stole our statue,
His sister helped him:
I accept God's words, I'm satisfied.

1480 Take them safely to Athens,
Let them honour our Lady there.
I'll send these women home to lovely Greece.
My warships, my soldiers
Swarming against these Greeks –
I call them back.
Athene, Lady, I hear and obey.

ATHENE.
You're wise. Fate rules us all,
Rules mortals and gods alike.
Winds, blow for Orestes, son of Agamemnon,
Waft him to Athens. I'll sail with him,
Keep guard on my sister's statue.

CHORUS.
1490 Home. Happiness. Blessings.
Fate smiles at last.
Lady, Athene, all honour:
Words of delight, of joy,
We hear and obey.

    *Exeunt.*

# APPENDIX

## 'Agamemnon's Children'

The decision to perform these three plays together, as a single experience, at the Gate Theatre in 1995, involved fewer changes than we originally expected. Apart from one or two small cuts in the bodies of the plays – Oiax (page 73), Danaos and Aigyptos (page 90) and Io (page 135) disappeared, for example – our main changes were at the beginning and end of each play. We took out inconsistencies in the prologues and the gods' speeches, making the myth as recounted harmonise with what happens in the other plays. The revised speeches are as follows:

## (1) **Elektra** (*l. 1*)

FARMER.
   Argos! Dazzle! Glory of Greece!
   From here, these streams, this plain,
   Lord Agamemnon sailed for Troy.
   Greece chose him, Grand Admiral,
   To lead the fleet that sailed for Helen,
   His brother's husband Helen, stolen by Trojans,
   Gods did it: they wanted war,
   Greeks against Trojans, they took Helen,
   Wife of Agamemnon's brother Menelaos,
   And gave her to Prince Paris of Troy.
   So Paris stole Helen. All Greece sent ships
   To fetch her back, Agamemnon Grand Admiral.
   They gathered at Aulis. A thousand ships.
   And the gods held back the winds.
   Agamemnon made sacrifice,
   Asked what to do, and the prophet said,
   'Majesty, warlord of Greece,
   You made a vow, years ago, to Artemis:
   You'd sacrifice to her
   The most beautiful thing in Argos.

Well, that most beautiful thing
Is your own daughter, Iphigeneia.
Your own and Klytemnestra's daughter.
If you want wind for your ships,
Take her, lord, sacrifice her,
Blood for the goddess. Your own hand: do it.'

So it began. He wept, Agamemnon,
Dashed his sceptre on the ground. God's orders:
No escape. He sent for his daughter,
Pretended she was going to her wedding,
With Achilles, glittering Achilles, Greek of Greeks –
And then on the altar, in Aulis, he cut her throat.
Agamemnon cut Iphigeneia's throat.
All Greece knows the story. All Greece heard –
Including Agamemnon's wife,
Iphigeneia's mother, Klytemnestra
At home in Argos. Hate filled her heart.

So Agamemnon sailed for Troy, sacked Troy,
That city of ancient kings, sailed home again,
Home again here, to Argos,
And piled our temples high with Trojan gold,
The splendour of the East. So far so good.
But then he died. Murdered. *She* killed him,
Klytemnestra his wife, held him in a scarlet net
While Aigisthos her lover chopped him down;
Like foresters, with an axe they ended him.
The king was dead, long live the king:
Aigisthos, Klytemnestra his consort.
There were two other children,
Klytemnestra's children, Agamemnon's children,
Left when he sailed to Troy. His son, Orestes;
Elektra, his daughter – a young girl, a little boy.
Aigisthos planned to kill Orestes
(The son and heir), but an old man,
Agamemnon's old tutor,
Who loved Orestes, loved him like a father,
Stole him away to Phokis, where he grew up
In the care of King Strophios, safe and sound.
(*continues l. 19*)

(2) **Elektra** (*l. 1238 to end*)

*Enter* KASTOR *and* POLYDEUKES. *Music ends.*

KASTOR.

Orestes, Prince of Argos, hear us. Zeus' sons,
Your mother's brothers, Kastor, Polydeukes,
Mortals once, now gods, our job to calm the sea.
We came to Argos. We watched you kill
Our sister, your mother. She deserved to die.
Apollo ordered it, but the guilt is yours,
Mortal murder, mortal guilt. Now hear
What Zeus and the Fates ordain for you.
There are Furies, your mother's Furies,
Born of her blood. They'll hunt you down.
No one else will hear them, see them:
It's you they want, your wits, your life.
Blood for blood, your life. Hear them,
Swarming, skins of darkness, snake-bracelets,
They'll sniff you out, it's now, it's now,
You're theirs!

*Music.*

CHORUS.

Lord. Son of Zeus. Hear us.

KASTOR.

Speak; you have no guilt in this.

CHORUS.

Klytemnestra's brothers.
You knew she was to die –
Why didn't you prevent it?

KASTOR.

Fate demanded it. Apollo ordered it.

ELEKTRA.

I had no orders.
God didn't order me to kill.

KASTOR.

You shared it: one crime,
One guilt, one madness.

ORESTES.
Elektra, I longed for you.
All these years, I needed you.

ELEKTRA.
Orestes, hold me.
Darling. We have to part.
Fate. Her blood. She's won.

ORESTES.
Hold me. Kiss me.
I'm dead: weep tears for me.

KASTOR.
Feoo feoo. This is very sad.
Gods weep for you. I weep.
For mortals, look! gods weep.

We're off now. Ships to protect.
We sail through the sky, we part the clouds,
For honest folk, not criminals.
If you're good, respect the law,
Respect the gods,
Don't ever go to sea with criminals,
We'll help you. Remember that. God speaks.

*Exeunt* KASTOR *and* POLYDEUKES.

CHORUS.
Sons of Zeus, farewell.
And may all of us fare well,
In the race of life, not stumble,
Run free at last, to happiness.

*Exeunt.*


(3) **Orestes** (*l. 1*)

ELEKTRA.
Disaster, pain, plague, misery,
Whatever the gods choose to heap on us –
The human condition. We shoulder it.
Agamemnon, for example,
Glorious Agamemnon, if glorious is the word.

And his brother Menelaos. (Not so glorious.)
Menelaos married Helen
(The one the gods detest),
And Agamemnon married her sister,
Klytemnestra – a catch, all Greece thought that.
Two girls they had – Iphigeneia,
Me (Elektra, yes) – and one boy, Orestes.
Agamemnon's children, and hers,
That bitch, that foulness,
Who wrapped her own husband in a woven net
And killed him. Why? She had her reasons,
She says she had her reasons. Married reasons.
I'm an innocent virgin, know nothing of marriage,
It's not for me to say, you work it out. (*continues l. 27*)

### (4) **Iphigeneia in Tauris** (*l. 77*)

ORESTES.
   It's a trap, Apollo, another trap. Why?
   I avenged my father, killed my mother,
   They haunt me, Furies, bloodhounds,
   Hunt me, no rest, whirling, whirling.
   'Go to Athens,' you said. 'Stand trial.'
   I went, I was acquitted, and then you said,
   'Not done. No rest, no ease, not done.
   Ends of the earth. Go there.
   Our Lady's shrine. Artemis, Apollo's sister. Go.
   Take the statue, it fell from the sky, they say,
   Find a way to steal it, take it to Athens, give it.'
   Just like that. 'It'll ease your pain,' you said.
   'A breathing-space,' you said. Well, I'm here.
   Ends of the earth. I've done all you asked.
   I'm here. There's no one. Now what? (*continues l. 96*)

# A Note on the Translator and Series Editor

KENNETH McLEISH's translations, of plays by all the Greek and Roman dramatists, Ibsen, Feydeau, Molière, Strindberg and others, have been performed throughout the world on stage, film, TV and radio. His original plays include *I Will If You Will*, *Just Do It*, *One for the Money*, *Omma* and *Orpheus*. His books include *The Theatre of Aristophanes*, *Guide to Shakespeare's Plays* (with Stephen Unwin), *The Good Reading Guide* and *Companion to the Arts in the Twentieth Century*. He is Editor of the Drama Classics series for Nick Hern Books.

J. MICHAEL WALTON worked in the professional theatre as an actor and director before joining the University of Hull, where he is Professor of Drama. He has published four books on Greek theatre, *Greek Theatre Practice*, *The Greek Sense of Theatre: Tragedy Reviewed*, *Living Greek Theatre: A Handbook of Classical Performance and Modern Production* and *Menander and the Making of Comedy* (with the late Peter Arnott). He edited *Craig on Theatre* for Methuen and is Series Editor of Methuen Classical Greek Dramatists. He has translated plays by Sophocles, Euripides, Menander and Terence and is Director of the Performance Translation Centre in the Drama Department at the University of Hull.

# Methuen World Classics *and*
# Methuen Contemporary Dramatists

Aeschylus (two volumes)
Jean Anouilh
John Arden (two volumes)
Arden & D'Arcy
Aristophanes (two volumes)
Aristophanes & Menander
Peter Barnes (three volumes)
Sebastian Barry
Brendan Behan
Aphra Behn
Edward Bond (five volumes)
Bertolt Brecht (six volumes)
Howard Brenton (two volumes)
Büchner
Bulgakov
Calderón
Jim Cartwright
Anton Chekhov
Caryl Churchill (two volumes)
Noël Coward (five volumes)
Sarah Daniels (two volumes)
Eduardo De Filippo
David Edgar (three volumes)
Euripides (three volumes)
Dario Fo (two volumes)
Michael Frayn (two volumes)
Max Frisch
Gorky
Harley Granville Barker
  (two volumes)
Peter Handke
Henrik Ibsen (six volumes)
Terry Johnson
Bernard-Marie Koltès

Lorca (three volumes)
David Mamet (three volumes)
Marivaux
Mustapha Matura
David Mercer (two volumes)
Arthur Miller (five volumes)
Anthony Minghella (two volumes)
Molière
Tom Murphy (four volumes)
Musset
Peter Nichols (two volumes)
Clifford Odets
Joe Orton
Philip Osment
Louise Page
A. W. Pinero
Luigi Pirandello
Stephen Poliakoff (two volumes)
Terence Rattigan
Christina Reid
Willy Russell
Ntozake Shange
Sam Shepard (two volumes)
Sophocles (two volumes)
Wole Soyinka
David Storey (two volumes)
August Strindberg (three volumes)
J. M. Synge
Sue Townsend
Ramón del Valle-Inclán
Frank Wedekind
Michael Wilcox
Oscar Wilde

# Methuen Modern Plays

*include work by*

Jean Anouilh
John Arden
Margaretta D'Arcy
Peter Barnes
Sebastian Barry
Brendan Behan
Edward Bond
Bertolt Brecht
Howard Brenton
Simon Burke
Jim Cartwright
Caryl Churchill
Noël Coward
Sarah Daniels
Nick Dear
Shelagh Delaney
David Edgar
Dario Fo
Michael Frayn
John Godber
Paul Godfrey
David Greig
John Guare
Peter Handke
Jonathan Harvey
Iain Heggie
Declan Hughes
Terry Johnson
Sarah Kane
Charlotte Keatley
Barrie Keeffe
Robert Lepage
Stephen Lowe

Doug Lucie
Martin McDonagh
John McGrath
David Mamet
Patrick Marber
Arthur Miller
Mtwa, Ngema & Simon
Tom Murphy
Phyllis Nagy
Peter Nichols
Joseph O'Connor
Joe Orton
Louise Page
Joe Penhall
Luigi Pirandello
Stephen Poliakoff
Franca Rame
Mark Ravenhill
Philip Ridley
Reginald Rose
David Rudkin
Willy Russell
Jean-Paul Sartre
Sam Shepard
Wole Soyinka
C. P. Taylor
Theatre de Complicite
Theatre Workshop
Sue Townsend
Judy Upton
Timberlake Wertenbaker
Victoria Wood

# Methuen Student Editions

For a Complete Catalogue of Methuen Drama titles
write to:

Methuen Drama
Random House
20 Vauxhall Bridge Road
London SW1V 2SA